11-30-22

FINDING
OUR WAY
AGAIN

THE RETURN
OF THE
ANCIENT
PRACTICES

BRIAN
MCLAREN

THOMAS NEL

Since 1798

D1023148

NASHVILLE   DALLAS   MEXICO CITY   RIO DE JANEIRO

Published in Nashville, Tennessee, by Thomas Nelson. Thomas Nelson is a registered trademark of Thomas Nelson, Inc.

Published in association with Kathryn A. Helmers, Helmers Literary Agency, PO Box 50737, Colorado Springs, CO 80949-0737.

Thomas Nelson, Inc. titles may be purchased in bulk for educational, business, fund-raising, or sales promotional use. For information, please e-mail SpecialMarkets@ThomasNelson.com.

ISBN 978-0-8499-4602-8 (trade paper)

Library of Congress Cataloging-in-Publication Data

McLaren, Brian D., 1956-
    Finding our way again : the return of the ancient practices/
Brian D. McLaren.
        p. cm.
    Includes bibliographical references and index.
    ISBN 978-0-8499-0114-0 (hardcover)
    1. Spirituality—History. 2. Spiritual direction–History. I. Title.
BV4490.M37 2008
248.4'6—dc22

                                                            2007049258

Printed in the United States of America

10 11 12 13 14 RRD 5 4 3 2 1

This book is dedicated to local church pastors and their spouses who are leading their congregations to rediscover the Christian faith as a transforming way of life. Your work is hard, I know. But it is worthwhile, and much depends on your courage, resilience, and creativity. This book is also dedicated to all who are involved in the New Monasticism (www.newmonasticism.org), and to all who will be inspired by their example, even if from a distance. You are leading the way.

CONTENTS

ACKNOWLEDGMENTS   vii
FOREWORD   viii
    CHAPTER 1:   SEARCHING FOR AN EVERYDAY SACREDNESS   1

PART 1: WAY

    CHAPTER 2:   WHY SPIRITUAL PRACTICES MATTER   11
    CHAPTER 3:   THE GENESIS OF PRACTICE   21
    CHAPTER 4:   PRACTICING THE WAY OF JESUS   31
    CHAPTER 5:   PAUL AND THE WAY OF LOVE   41
    CHAPTER 6:   SHARING TREASURES AMONG FRIENDS   51
    CHAPTER 7:   OPEN-SOURCE SPIRITUALITY   61
    CHAPTER 8:   SHALLOW TROUBLE, DEEP TROUBLE   67

PART 2: PRACTICES

    CHAPTER 9:   PRACTICE MAKES POSSIBLE   79
  CHAPTER 10:   CONTEMPLATIVE PRACTICES   89
  CHAPTER 11:   COMMUNAL PRACTICES   99
  CHAPTER 12:   MISSIONAL PRACTICES   113
  CHAPTER 13:   THE CYCLE WE FIND OURSELVES IN   123
  CHAPTER 14:   MOVING ON   131

PART 3: ANCIENT

  CHAPTER 15:   PRACTICING THE ANCIENT WAY   143
  CHAPTER 16:   KATHARSIS (VIA PURGATIVA)   151
  CHAPTER 17:   FOTOSIS (VIA ILLUMINATIVA)   159
  CHAPTER 18:   THEOSIS (VIA UNITIVA)   169
  CHAPTER 19:   FAITHING OUR PRACTICES   181
  CHAPTER 20:   LEARNING BY (BROKEN) HEART   191

    STUDY GUIDE   205
          NOTES   213
ABOUT THE AUTHOR   223

ACKNOWLEDGMENTS

I am indebted in a special way to Dallas Willard, Richard Foster, Eugene Peterson, and Joan Chittister; their writings introduced me to the contemplative life and the idea of spiritual disciplines or practices.[1] I am similarly indebted to Tony Campolo, Jim Wallis, and Ron Sider; their works introduced me to the integration of the contemplative life and a life of social action.[2]

And I am no less indebted to friends with whom I have experienced the communal life, which integrates the contemplative and active ways. From them I have learned more than I can put into words—especially through Cedar Ridge Community Church (crcc.org) and the emergent community (emergentvillage.com). At Cedar Ridge, one of my great joys has been watching Patsy Fratanduono and Melanie Griffin begin as fledgling disciples and grow to lead others in the way of Christ, embodying the practices this book tries to describe. They call me a mentor, but I now feel I learn more from them. I remember the first time I experienced *lectio divina*, guided by Tony Jones, and body prayer, guided by Doug Pagitt. It's been a joy to watch Diana Butler Bass open up the world of spiritual practices for new communities of readers.[3] They and so many others have created and enhanced for me the kind of safe space in which the best learning best takes place.

FOREWORD

As a rule, forewords, when they occur at all, speak their truth about one particular volume of work and only one. Having been always just slightly less than compliant by disposition, though, there is a kind of perverse joy for me every time I find a way to violate such a rule both with impunity and to good purpose, which is why I think you probably need to know right up front that as I write this foreword, I am joyful.

Most of us know, either by instinct or by deliberate investigation, that Christianity is going through a time of enormous upheaval. When last our faith went through such a dramatic and total reconfiguration, we gave our reshuffling the portentous name of the Great Reformation. Now the church is changing again, working and chafing under the heat of severe cultural shifts and earthquakes.

One thing is certain, nevertheless: some of us are sure we don't like it. Others are more sanguine and assume the whole thing will settle down in God's good time without requiring any particular engagement on their part. And a few of us look at what is happening as the old denominations falter and nondenominational communities increase and as worship becomes more passionate and communal and incarnational, and are ready to say, "Ah, there's a new movement of the Spirit among us, a new form of the kingdom, a new understanding of vocation and its totality." Young men and women of faith, especially, are crying everywhere, "Give us a faith that costs us something! We want to feel the passion of those who knew and know Christianity is worth dying for! Teach us the things that will mark us as children of God! Make of us a holy nation before our God!"

Their demands swell out with heat and vision, and what they foretell is that Christianity must be a way of living life as much as it is a system of belief. What they envision are Christians who belong to each other in common cause, regardless of place and circumstance, a tribe of people marked by how they are and live as a nation peculiar unto God, regardless of where they may exist on this earth. It is a soul-shaking concept. Yet, it is as old as the Judaism out of which we come and in terms of which we Christians see ourselves as inheritors of an eternal promise.

Such battle cries have not been heard for a while, at least not in most of the first world. They startle, offend, and accuse—and they also pierce. But regardless of where one is in the wide family of Christian affiliation, it is impossible not to discern that their demands also come bearing blessings for the whole body of Christ on earth assembled.

That is why the entire church is being forced to prayerfully re-examine the character and practices of our ancient forefathers and foremothers in the faith. We must begin again, as once our forebears did, to live not as culturally safe Christians, but as observant ones, the markings of our faith becoming so inherent in each of us as to be the faith incarnated in us. We must, in other words, find our way again—and thus the title of this book.

In its pages and in its lines of lucid argument, Brian McLaren writes a no-holds-barred overview of both the grandeur and the odium of living fully Christian in a post-Christendom society. He underscores the necessity for that commitment and revisits the means by which Christians and Jews have always dared to fashion themselves before God. What he has to say will not persuade all of us, but it should unsettle every one of us, accusing us each and every one of being less then we must be, and inspiring us with the hope that still there is time, that still we can strive toward fuller citizenship.

What McLaren does in these pages, in other words, is to brilliantly lay before us an absolute call for every practicing Christian to assume the characteristic faith-marking ways of our spiritual elders.

So then, in writing the foreword to his book, I am doing two things. First and most gratefully, I am taking advantage of an opportunity to praise a piece of work and a religious posture that I passionately believe in. But I have another purpose as well. With equal gratitude, I am using this foreword as a way to introduce a whole series of books for which the present one serves as both the first of eight volumes and as the context for them all.

Those books are listed, along with the names of their authors, on the fly leaf of this volume. As you will see from their titles, each of the seven outstanding books is concerned not with a theory of spiritual discipline, as is this one, but rather with a particular and specific spiritual practice. In aggregate, these, with McLaren's persuasive *Finding Our Way Again – The Return of the Ancient Practices*, illustrate seven ancient ways of spiritual and religious formation that have shaped the Abrahamic faiths from the beginning of time. I believe that they will evoke in each of us a prayerful reconsideration of how Christians are called to live, as well as to believe.

And that, in sum, is why I am, with joy, signing my name here.

Phyllis Tickle
General Editor
Ancient Practices Series

CHAPTER 1

SEARCHING FOR AN EVERYDAY SACREDNESS

It was one of those moments of panic that gets translated into anxiety dreams—the kind where you're trying to run, but your legs feel like a mixture of lead and rubber, or where you're transported back in time to a hallway in your high school, and you look down to realize you forgot to put on your pants, or where you're trying to catch a train, but your suitcase falls open, and your clothes pour out on the platform.

I was at a conference for pastors, where I had been asked to introduce a famous speaker, Dr. Peter Senge. I had come well prepared, because at the time I was in my thirties and quite fearful of doing anything less than excellently. So it puzzled me that in the days leading up to Dr. Senge's presentation, the event organizer, Brad, kept quizzing me: "Hey, Brian—ready for your big day on Thursday?" *Why is he so anxious about my introduction?* I thought. *Either I'm a liability, or he's a control freak.* The night before the big day, Brad nudged me one more time. "So, Brian, you're sure you're ready to interview Dr. Senge tomorrow, right?"

That's the moment when the real-life anxiety dream began. *Interview Dr. Senge?* I thought to myself in panic. *But I thought I was only supposed to* introduce *him*. It didn't matter how the misunder-standing had occurred. Ready or not, I was on for the big event.

"Sure thing, Brad," I responded casually. Trying to appear calm, I beat a hasty retreat to my room, frantically pulled out a yellow pad, and began scribbling possible questions. Dr. Senge was sched-uled to appear from a remote location via satellite teleconference, which only made the task more daunting.

The next day I arrived at the lecture hall a half hour early and went over timing with Brad and his team. Then, predictably, there was a "bug" in the satellite hookup, so I soon found myself stand-ing in front of the crowd next to a large screen filled with static, fill-ing in time. I could see someone in the production booth making exaggerated gestures at me, pulling apart the fingertips of his two hands in a kind of taffy-stretching motion. I ran through my planned introduction about Dr. Senge being one of the fathers of systems thinking. Then I began to improvise, describing how his book *The Fifth Discipline* had influenced my thinking as a pastor, and so on, and so on.

Just as I was about to break into a couple of dance steps to entertain the crowd, the satellite hookup was completed. I looked down at my yellow legal pad and stumbled into one of the lamest opening questions ever asked: "Hello, Dr. Senge. It's a great honor for us to have you with us. Your image is being projected to about five hundred pastors. I imagine this is a different kind of crowd than you normally address. What would you like to say to a group of five hundred Christian ministers?"

Dr. Senge's gracious response compensated for my nervousness: "Well, Brian, you're right. I don't normally speak to pastors. Actually, I was thinking about that very question yesterday when I was in a large bookstore. I asked the bookstore manager what the most popular books are these days. Most popular, he said, were books about how to get rich in the new information economy, which didn't surprise me."

A ripple of laughter gave me a moment of relief. Dr. Senge continued, "Second most popular, the manager said, were books about spirituality, and in particular, books about Buddhism. And so when I thought about speaking to five hundred Christian pastors today, I thought I'd begin by asking you all a question: why are books on Buddhism so popular, and not books on Christianity?"

Great. Not only did I have to pose questions to a face on the screen, but now I had to field one from him as well. I managed to recover enough to punt the question back to him. "Well, Dr. Senge," I said, trying not to sound as clumsy as I felt, "how would *you* answer that question?"

He replied, "I think it's because Buddhism presents itself as a way of life, and Christianity presents itself as a system of belief. So I would want to get Christian ministers thinking about how to rediscover their own faith as a way of life, because that's what people are searching for today. That's what they need most."

I don't remember a single thing about the rest of the interview, but I will always remember Dr. Senge's statement. In fact, a number of the attendees told me how that one statement was worth the price of the entire event for them. In the days and weeks after the event, I couldn't stop thinking about the relative proportions we in our religious communities had assigned to "system of belief" and to "way of life." And I couldn't help but agree with Dr. Senge: we must rediscover our faith as a way of life, not simply as a system of belief.

The issue, of course, isn't either/or, but both/and; it's hard to deny that too many of us have lost the "way" of our faith. Without a coherent and compelling way of life, formed in community and expressed in mission, some of us begin losing interest in the system of belief, or we begin holding it grimly, even meanly, driving more and more people away from our faith rather than attracting them toward it.

Those who reject religion are often rejecting a certain arid system of belief, or if not that, a set of trivial taboos or rules or rituals that have lost meaning for them—each the thin residue of a lost way of life.

However, in this age of environmental unsustainability, the unconscionable juxtaposition between wasteful luxury and crushing poverty, and intensifying conflicts that can avalanche into potentially catastrophic war, nearly everyone, whether nonreligious or religious, seems to agree that we need to discover or rediscover a viable way of life. Much of what we'll explore in this series of books will involve restoring a kind of sacred normalcy to the rhythms of life—making prayer ordinary in our daily schedule or annual calendar; making generosity normal, normative, and habitual so that it is done automatically; making regular time for rest every single week whether we feel we need it or not, as a matter of routine; practicing simplicity instead of consumption; countering violence with peacemaking.

If the modern era can be characterized by a cold war between scientific and religious belief systems, then the postmodern era can best be characterized by a search for *spirituality*, a word that somehow captures this idea of a viable, sustainable, meaningful way of life. After centuries of a relationship almost always characterized by the term *versus*, the scientific and religious communities seem to realize that we need to move beyond our deadlock, our polarization, our binary, either/or thinking regarding faith and reason, religion and science, matter and spirit.

The word *spiritual* captures this reintegration for us; it says, "We don't believe that conventional organized religion has all the answers for us, nor does secular, reductionist science. We need a fusion of the sacred and the secular. We need an everyday sacredness." The word *spirituality* tries to capture that fusion of everyday sacredness. For many people, it represents a life-giving alternative to secularist fundamentalism and religious fundamentalism, the former offering the world weapons of mass destruction and the latter stirring emotions to put the suicidal machinery into motion.

Our story (in the West, at least) could be told like this: we are witnessing the transition from conventional premodern religions, to an early modern period of institutional religion, to a late-modern religious collapse and replacement by secularism, to a growing dissatisfaction with all of the above—premodern religion, institutional religion, and modern secularism. This dissatisfaction in some cases has led to a reactionary resurgence of pushy fundamentalism—fearful, manic, violent, apocalyptic. And in other cases it has led to a search for a new kind of spirituality. The success or failure of this search will, no doubt, play a major role in the story of the twenty-first century.

In its early stages, this search for spirituality has been associated with the term *new age,* which for many means something vague, consumerist, undefined, and mushy. However, in the aftermath of September 11, 2001, more and more of us are realizing that a warm but mushy spirituality is no match for hot and pushy fundamentalism, of whatever religious variety, especially when that fundamentalism is well armed, dangerous, and in the mood for an apocalypse. More and more of us feel, more and more intensely, the need for a fresh, creative alternative—a fourth alternative, something beyond militarist scientific secularism, pushy religious fundamentalism, and mushy amorphous spirituality.

This alternative, we realize, needs to be creative and new to face the new challenges of a new age, a world gone "post-al"—

postmodern, postcolonial, post-Enlightenment, post-Christendom, post-Holocaust, post-9/11. Yet it also needs to derive strength from the old religious traditions; it needs to face new-age challenges with age-old wisdom. The challenge of the future will require, we realize, rediscovery and adaptive reuse of resources from the ancient past.

This book—together with the series of books it introduces—explores this fresh alternative, this fourth way beyond three unacceptable alternatives. It seeks to bring ancient spiritual practices to bear on the emerging world. It reaches toward an alternative beyond a reductionistic secularism, beyond a reactive and intransigent fundamentalism, and beyond a vague, consumerist spirituality.

This new focus is an acknowledgment that we have lost the path and are seeking to rediscover our faith as a way of life, shaped and strengthened by ancient practices. Although written by a Christian primarily for Christians, this initial book in the series extends our acknowledgment to unreligious people as well as to adherents of all three Abrahamic faiths: Judaism, Christianity, and Islam. Each of the books following this one in the series will explore in depth and detail one of the seven ancient practices shared by the Abrahamic faith traditions: fixed-hour prayer, fasting, Sabbath, the sacred meal, pilgrimage, observance of sacred seasons, and giving.

SPIRITUAL EXERCISES

1. Using the matrix below, plot your life in five-year increments. For example, when you were five years old, was your faith more a way of life or a system of belief, or was it low on both counts? How about at fifteen? Twenty-five? Where would you like it to be for five–year increments into the future?

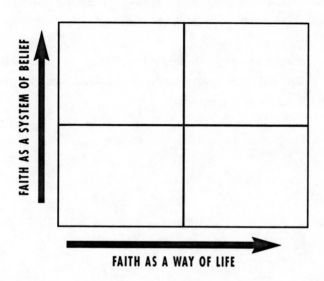

2. Imagine yourself in the cold war between science and religion described in this chapter. Which side have you been on? Or have you been caught in the crossfire? Describe your experience and how this war has affected you or people close to you.

3. Reflect on the ideas of a "fusion between the sacred and the secular" and "everyday sacredness." Describe your experiences of this kind of fusion, and then describe your aspirations or hopes for it. What would it mean for you to learn how to live in this kind of fusion?

4. Consider the three common religious alternatives described in this chapter: scientific secularism, "hot and pushy fundamentalism," and "warm but mushy spirituality." Name strengths and weaknesses of each, and then imagine combining the strengths into a fourth alternative.

5. Give yourself permission to write in this book (unless it's borrowed

from the library or a friend). Underline. Write notes in the margins. Ask questions. Jot down ideas. Talk back. Make this book a two-way conversation.

6. Go over your answers to questions one through four above. Say (or better, write) a prayer that expresses your hopes, desires, dreams, concerns, and decisions

PART 1
WAY

C H A P T E R 2

You can't take an epidural shot to ease the pain of giving birth to character. In a sense, every day of your life is labor: the rhythmic agony
of producing the person who will wake up in your body tomorrow,
creating your reputation, continuing your legacy, and influencing
your family, friends, colleagues, neighbors, and countless strangers,
for better or worse. It is questionable whether you can ever be exactly
the same person for two consecutive days: what today throws at you
will force you to become better
or bitter for tomorrow; it will
push you toward breakdown or
breakthrough, nudge you a step
closer to courage, nobility,
charity, integrity, and honor . . .
or otherwise.

> **YOU CAN'T TAKE AN
> EPIDURAL SHOT TO EASE
> THE PAIN OF GIVING BIRTH
> TO CHARACTER.**

In a wild world like ours,
your character, left untended,
will become a stale room, an
obnoxious child, a vacant lot

11

filled with thorns, weeds, broken bottles, raggedy grocery bags, and dog droppings. Your deepest channels will silt in, and you will feel yourself shallowing. You'll become a presence neither you nor others will enjoy, and you and they will spend more and more time and energy trying to be anywhere else.

Well tended, your character will be a fragrant garden, an artist's home, with walls and halls full of memories and beauty, a party with live music and good jokes and pleasant conversations in every corner. You'll be good and deep company for others and yourself.

That's why, through the ages, people have tried to find ways to tend themselves, to do for their souls what exercise does for their bodies or study for their minds. Through these character exercises, they give birth to the person they are proud of becoming, the person they are happy to be, the one who is trying to be born in them every day—a hero, a best friend, a loving beloved and beloved lover.

This might sound wonderful, and it is, but it works itself out in the mess, drudgery, stress, triviality, trauma, perplexity, and hilarity of odd days and traffic jams—the kinds of things that have happened to you in the last two days, or will happen in the next two. You know. It's that time of month, and your wife is really grouchy, or your husband is complaining about bills again. Your boss is having a torrid affair with the company accountant, which means his mind isn't on his work, which means that things are chaotic at the office, and you're stuck with the mess. You don't know it, but your son is planning to call you tomorrow to tell you he's gay or getting divorced or in trouble with the law or running for governor. Or your husband will lose his job next Friday, or your grandchild will be diagnosed with autism next month, or your air conditioner will break down the morning of the hottest day in twenty-five years, or your government is planning to drop bombs on another country right before the elections. How will these experiences form you?

What kind of person will you become in the math and aftermath of all the fecality life slings at you between diapers and Depends?

Maybe you're one of the fortunate ones for whom everything goes well, for whom success and popularity keep dropping like coins into your hands, and for whom life's pain (so far) is easily treatable with regular-strength aspirin. Vodka, heroin, morphine, or plans for a mysterious disappearance have never once winked in your direction. You are no doubt thankful for your good fortune, but somewhere in the back of your mind you know: in terms of depth and character, a long stint of success and comfort may be the toughest test of all. Thirty years pass, and you've become just another greasy fast-food restaurant where the menu is full of lukewarm entrées under a purplish heat lamp: complacency, pride, ingratitude, superiority, apathy, cowardice, starch, fat, confectioner's sugar. You develop the habit of expressing your opinions whether others ask for them or not, or perhaps you realize that you actually don't have many opinions, and people think you're somewhat nice but have trouble remembering your name. You have become weightless, so any wind can blow you away. It's ironic, isn't it? Our bodies grow fatter, we're all on diets, and our souls, meanwhile, go wispy and anorexic.

> **SPIRITUAL PRACTICES ARE ACTIONS WITHIN OUR POWER THAT HELP US NARROW THE GAP. THEY HELP US BECOME SOMEONE WEIGHTY.**

Both the strugglers and the comfortable, then, need to mind the gap between the character they want to have and the character they are actually developing, which is reason number 1 for investing energy in a book like this. Spiritual practices are actions within our power that help us narrow the gap. They help us become someone weighty, someone worthy of a name and reputation, someone who makes survival worthwhile by turning life's manure into fertilizer. They're about surviving your twenties or forties or eighties and not becoming a jerk in the process. About not letting what happens to us deform us or destroy us. About realizing that what we earn or accumulate means nothing compared to what we become and who we are. As such, spiritual practices are pretty earthy, and they're not strictly about *spirituality* as it is often defined; they're about humanity. Which brings us to the second reason they're important—*aliveness*.

> SPIRITUAL PRACTICES COULD BE CALLED *LIFE PRACTICES* OR *HUMANE PRACTICES*, BECAUSE THEY HELP US PRACTICE BEING ALIVE, AND HUMANELY SO.

Spiritual practices could be called *life practices* or *humane practices*, because they help us practice being alive, and humanely so. They develop not just character but also aliveness, alertness, wakefulness, and humanity.

The sheer value of being alive seems to be what keeps us getting up after our last stupid mistake or heartbreaking disappointment or shattering trauma or surprising success, thinking, *Okay, now that's behind me. Let's get on with life. What's next?* The word *life* represents a mystery to us every moment we say it, feel it, and want more of it.

The awareness and mystery of life hit me one morning, on the last day in February. There was a little snow left on the ground from a storm a week earlier in Maryland, where I live. In spite of the cold, some of the birds had been singing their spring songs for about two weeks, an act of faith to greet each chilly dawn, maybe even an attempt to warm it up. I could hear them indistinctly from my kitchen.

I put on my jacket and stepped out in my backyard to pick out more clearly the songs I've come to know. No robins singing yet, although I heard their *pert-pert-perts* a few times and saw them hanging out in the naked trees, like teenagers smoking and joking before school. There was a white-throated sparrow singing (a kind of six-toned whistle, a little mournful, that makes me think of children swinging on a swing set), a cardinal (a stronger whistle—an ascending half note, a descending half note, followed by four ascending quarter notes), a house finch (a happy chatter that sounds like a complex sentence in a language humans can't yet understand), and a glorious Carolina wren (a whistle full of spurts, starts, and stops).

I wanted to get a glimpse of the wren, so I grabbed my binoculars and, after about five minutes, found him, snug against the trunk on a small branch high, high up, easy to miss. As I centered him in my view, I saw his buff brown chest puffing, his head turning left, right, and then up to sing. That mystery and awareness of aliveness suddenly pinged in my brain like a crystal glass struck by a dinner knife. A singing Carolina wren can become, if one listens and looks in the right way, a burning bush in which the divine is dancing like a flame.

This awareness kept pinging, dancing, and glowing with decreasing intensity that day as I went to the airport to fly halfway around the world, first from DC to LA, then overnight from LA to Hong Kong. Somewhere over the dark Pacific, the mystery had completely abandoned me, probably because I was flying in economy class, where few good things can long survive. By morning, catching my last flight from Hong Kong to Kuala Lumpur, my neck hurt, and I felt greasy and cross, and the mystery of life didn't impress me much. The Carolina wren of happiness was long forgotten.

> SPIRITUAL PRACTICES ARE ABOUT LIFE, ABOUT TRAINING OURSELVES TO BECOME THE KINDS OF PEOPLE WHO HAVE EYES AND ACTUALLY SEE, AND WHO HAVE EARS AND ACTUALLY HEAR, AND SO EXPERIENCE . . . NOT JUST SURVIVAL BUT *LIFE*.

Then, as the flight attendants were serving the obligatory scrambled-eggs breakfast, I looked groggily across the aisle: a couple and their two children were stirring. Mom and Dad had a well-behaved boy of about three and a tiny girl in a pink blanket—exactly six weeks old, I heard the mother tell the flight attendant, adding that the baby had come two months premature, which sort of made her minus-two weeks old. Over the next few hours, I watched Dad care for the boy, putting together some miniature LEGOs, taking in a video about penguins, guiding him down the long aisle to the restroom a couple of times. Then, just before landing, I watched Mom and baby stare into each other's eyes, mirroring smiles and wide-eyed giggles, two separate persons who couldn't be more connected even if the umbilical cord were still intact, and there was the mystery again. Life—pinging, singing, dancing, glowing, even in the cheap seats.

SPIRITUAL PRACTICES ARE WAYS OF BECOMING AWAKE AND STAYING AWAKE TO GOD.

That's why I say that spiritual practices are about life, about training ourselves to become the kinds of people who have eyes and actually see, and who have ears and actually hear, and so experience—with increasing consistency and resiliency, even in economy class—not just survival but *Life*, capitalized and modified by insufficient adjectives such as *real, abundant, examined, conscious, worth living,* and *good.*

In these two ways, then, paying attention to "life practices" is worthwhile for everybody, those who consider themselves spiritual and those who don't: first, because nobody wants to become a tedious fart, and second, because nobody wants to miss Life because they're short on legroom and sleep in economy class.

I haven't told the whole story though. Yes, spiritual practices are ways of exercising intention regarding the kinds of people we are becoming at every turn. Yes, they are ways of habitually waking up and discovering Life. But the capitalization of Life points beyond life itself: spiritual practices are also and truly about the Spirit. They are about somehow driving with our windows wide open to God, keeping our elbows in the wind and our hands surfing beside the side mirror.

They're about tuning our radios to the frequency of the Holy, turning up the volume, and then daring to sing along. They're about staying alert so our eyes see the glory of the coming of the Lord, and our ears hear the Word, and our skin feels the warm touch and the gentle pressure of the Presence. (As we will see, spiritual practices are also about being sustained through the perceived absence of the Presence.)

Spiritual practices are a way of putting the universe on fast-rewind until it collapses into a singularity of dark light, so as to recall that all creation originally unfolded from the divine source singing, "Let there be . . ." They are, likewise, a way of putting the universe on fast-forward, imagining it hurtling forward and outward until it is caught up in the wide arms of grace—like a beginning toddler falling with awkward, joyous determination across space toward his mother's arms. And perhaps most important, they are a way of locating ourselves in a present moment no less lighted by the presence of the unseen God from whom we come, to whom we go, and with whom we travel.

Spiritual practices are ways of becoming awake and staying awake to God—that's the third reason.

Perhaps, you say, that should go first—we should talk about spiritual formation as being first and foremost about the experience of God, and second about the formation of character, and then thirdly about the sustenance of wakefulness to life. Perhaps you're right. But perhaps the three can't be so easily separated. Perhaps the kind of person you are becoming determines how much of God you can experience—and maybe even which version of God you experience. Perhaps the acuity of your perception determines whether the signs catch your attention enough to signify for you anything divine or whether the wonders get your attention long enough to set you to wondering.

So for these three reasons, plus one more we'll address in closing, spiritual practices can help reshape us for a more intentional, attentive, and perceptive way of living. But that doesn't explain why *ancient* practices should have a special appeal. For a lot of people, the word *ancient* evokes dust and mildew, cobwebs and mummies. It marries the sexy, young word *spiritual* to the stodgy, middle-aged word *religious*. If you're in the market for spiritual practices, why prefer ancient ones over the latest ones? That will become clear within a few chapters.

SPIRITUAL EXERCISES

CHARACTER

1. Think about who you were yesterday in terms of character, compared to who you are today. How would you fill in these blanks: "Today I'm more . . . and less . . . than yesterday"? Do the same regarding a year ago and ten years ago.
2. What will your character be like in ten years, given your current trajectory.
3. Based on how you answered question number two, if necessary, cry. If possible, celebrate. Write down one step you want to take in response to how you answered question number two.

ALIVENESS

1. Are you awake? What have you missed—in terms of sights, sounds, feelings, smells, and so on—in the last five minutes? The last twenty-four hours? Slow down and be aware of any "Carolina wrens of happiness" that surround you at this moment.
2. Rate yourself on a scale of one to one hundred on how alive you feel at the present moment. A high score isn't the goal; an honest

score is. When was the last time you felt less than thirty? More than ninety?

3. What are the advantages of sleepwalking through life? What are the advantages of being alive and awake while your life happens?

EXPERIENCING GOD

1. If your relationship with God was a marriage, how would you describe things to a marriage counselor? What would a better, happier marriage look like?

2. If you pray, talk to God about your previous answers. If you don't normally pray, try it now. Many people find it helps either to write your prayer as a letter or actually pray out loud. If you want to try praying out loud but are afraid people will think you've tipped over the sanity ledge, you might find that taking a walk in the woods or hiding out in your car will give you some space and time.

CHAPTER 3

FIXED-HOUR PRAYER

Fixed-hour prayer, fasting, Sabbath, the sacred meal, pilgrimage, observance of sacred seasons, giving—all seven of the ancient spiritual practices are common to the major Abrahamic traditions of faith.

The largest religion in today's world is Christianity, accounting (loosely speaking) for about 33 percent of the world's inhabitants. Islam, the world's second-largest religion, accounts for an additional 20 percent, and both religions are daughters of Judaism. Together, these three religions nurture and guide more than half the world's population. And of course, they wield an influence that affects 100 percent of the planet's six-plus billion living human beings,

AT THE FOUNTAINHEAD OF THESE THREE RELIGIONS WE FIND A SINGLE FIGURE, AT ONCE FAMOUS AND MYSTERIOUS, A MIDDLE EASTERN MAN NAMED ABRAHAM OF UR.

not to mention the uncounted trillions of human beings who will someday exist unless aggressive and suicidal elements in these three religions drive us to extinction. No doubt, much of the influence of these religions is positive, but these days, many of us are worried that any two of the three of them could get us all nuked.

If we have, indeed, lost our way in the clamor of conflicting systems of belief, perhaps we can rediscover within our religious traditions some undervalued treasures they have in common. Christianity, Islam, and Judaism have more in common than many people realize because they all share a primal narrative, and they all flow from a common sacred fountainhead: a single figure, at once famous and mysterious, a Middle Eastern man named Abraham of Ur.

We can date Abraham's birth to about 2000 BC, in modern-day Iraq, near present-day Nasarif.[1] Like Moses, Jesus, and Muhammad—and like us—Abraham was raised in a pluralistic, polytheistic world. During his lifetime, he lived side by side with others who honored many different gods and practiced many different religions. And during his lifetime, Abraham—like Moses, Jesus, and Muhammad—had an encounter with God that distinguished him from his contemporaries and propelled him into a mission, introducing a new way of life that changed the world.

There is much we could say about Abraham, but for our purposes two incidents stand out, beginning with God's call to Abraham.

> Now the LORD said to Abram, "Go from your country and your kindred and your father's house to the land that I will show you. I will make of you a great nation, and I will bless you, and make your name great, so that you will be a blessing. I will bless those who bless you, and the one who curses you I will curse; and in you all the families of the earth shall be blessed."
>
> So Abram went, as the LORD had told him. (Genesis 12:1–4 NSRV)

How appropriate that the three Abrahamic religions begin with a journey into the unknown. It might be said that ever since, each religion has been at its best when it is on a journey, not settled on the throne of power at the capital city of Empire, but walking intrepid on a path of exploration to the margins of Empire and then beyond. Comfort and power can become great enemies of true spirituality and true humanity, which explains why we often say that the prophets come not only to comfort the afflicted but also to afflict the comfortable.

Now, I'm about to talk about the dangers of comfort, but before and after doing so, there is much to be said in praise of comfort, of normalcy, of routine, of ordinariness. When one of my sons was diagnosed with cancer and our lives were thrown into chaos, I remember feeling a poignant homesickness for a normal day, the way things used to be. People stricken by disease or accident look forward simply to coming home from the hospital to experience the most mundane things: sitting in their old, comfortable chairs; sleeping in their own beds; making a cup of coffee at their own counter in their own kitchen; petting their dogs and giving them their food. Similarly, in a time of war, distant memories of ordinariness are almost indistinguishable from the profound longing for peace.

HOW APPROPRIATE THAT THE THREE ABRAHAMIC RELIGIONS BEGIN WITH A JOURNEY INTO THE UNKNOWN.

Routine, regularity, normalcy, habit, ordinariness . . . these are as essential for the spiritual life as regular breathing, drinking, sleeping, and eating are for the physical life. But even so, a human body that is fed and rested regularly but doesn't engage in adequate exercise or stretching or movement will inevitably experience stiffness, lethargy, obesity, atrophy, and a host of even more serious diseases. So people of faith have periodically interrupted their normal lives with an intentional experience of discomfort, dislocation, and intensity, a kind of reenactment of the original journey of Abraham, by engaging in voluntary pilgrimage.

THEY SEEK

THE NEW, UNKNOWN PLACES

GOD WILL SHOW THEM

Like Abraham, they interrupt their participation in Empire by leaving their profit-making enterprises. They interrupt their normal family lives by breaking with the patriarchy of "father and father's house." They interrupt their normal orientations—the familiar sights and sounds of daily life—by seeking the new, unknown places God will show them. Whether they're Jews visiting Jerusalem, Muslims on Hajj to Mecca, or Christians going to Bethlehem, Lourdes, Rome, a retreat center, a youth camp, or a conference, the pilgrimage becomes for them a revival, a new birth, a rite of literal passage.

There is a second way people of faith interrupt regularity and normalcy: through fasting. What is more normal and regular for us than eating three meals a day? What is more habitual and routine than our personal or social customs of coffee and toast, sandwich and soft drink, meat and potatoes, rice and beans? To forgo normal eating—whether through a complete fast or through a partial fast—becomes a kind of dietary pilgrimage, a way of making sure we haven't let the rhythms of the everyday put us to sleep, a way to make sure that our habits have not become addictions, that our kitchens have not become prisons. Whether associated with Lent, Ramadan, or Yom Kippur, fasting is an exercise in extraordinary intentionality.

But again, there would be nothing extraordinary if there weren't a baseline of the ordinary to compare it to. There would be no syncopation if there were no steady rhythm, no pilgrimage if there were no home from which to set out or destination to reach, no holiday if there weren't a typical workweek. So just as the three Abrahamic faiths interrupt normalcy through pilgrimage and fasting, they try to create a better normalcy through other practices drawn from Abraham and his descendants.

Some of those regular practices emerge in Abraham's encounter with a mysterious figure known as the priest of Salem, King Melchizedek. In a sense, King Melchizedek represents "the other." He is not a member of Abraham's family or culture, nor is he a member of Abraham's religion (to the degree that Abraham could be said at this point even to have a religion). Even here, perhaps, in the otherness of Abraham and Melchizedek, there is a lesson for us: that we discover practices for our own faith in an encounter with someone of another faith who comes to us, not with argument or attack, but with blessing and hospitality:

> And King Melchizedek of Salem brought out bread and wine; he
> was priest of God Most High. He blessed him and said,
>   "Blessed be Abram by God Most High,
>   maker of heaven and earth;
>   and blessed be God Most High,
>   who has delivered your enemies into your hand!"
> And Abram gave him one-tenth of everything.
> (Genesis 14:18–20 NRSV)

If the first two Abrahamic practices are pilgrimage and fasting, the third is the holy meal, epitomized in the bread and wine shared by Abraham and Melchizedek. Later this meal will take the form of the Passover for Jews, the Eucharist for Christians, and Eid ul-Adha or Eid ul-Fitr for Muslims.[2] Interestingly, this primal meal wasn't intended as an expression of exclusion—just for Salemites or Abrahamics. It was a meal of peace and fellowship, bringing together two different people with their different religious traditions. The sacred meal in this light becomes a celebration of hospitality, of community, of inclusion, and of reconciliation.

The fourth Abrahamic practice is suggested in Melchizedek's prayer of blessing. Formalized prayers—prayers composed with intention and poetic sensibility—are essential to all Abrahamic faiths, and over time, they are integrated with the daily routine as fixed-hour prayer. This daily regimen of prayer is significant not only because it fills each day with regular times of turning the heart toward God, but also because the words of the prayers are constant and shared among the community. Fixed-hour prayer is common prayer, or communal prayer. Even though people pray in many places, they know they are expressing and affirming and being formed by those common desires, as individuals and as a community.

The fifth Abrahamic practice, proportional giving or tithing, also emerges in this passage. Abraham responds to Melchizedek's hospitality and blessing with a tenth of his "income."[3] Similarly, faithful people have made generosity habitual by giving at regular intervals in regular proportions. Some of this giving sustains priestly people such as King Melchizedek, people whose lives are devoted to sustaining the spiritual life of the people who give. Some is directed toward the poor, those who are so easily forgotten and marginalized. Through this spiritual practice, the poor are perpetually brought to remembrance and are given a place in the community not as parasites or losers, but as honored members of the family, members worthy of care.[4]

The last two Abrahamic practices arise among the patriarch's descendants. Abraham settles in Canaan, where he has, late in life, a son named Isaac. Isaac has a son named Jacob (aka Israel). Jacob's son Joseph ends up (through a long and harrowing story, beyond our scope here) in Egypt, and later, due to a famine in the land of Canaan, his brothers join him in Egypt as refugees. Sadly, the temporary refugees are detained and reduced to slavery in the Egyptian empire. About four hundred years pass, and Moses (about 1400 BC) arises as their liberator and leads them (another long and harrowing story) out of Egypt, into the desert, and to the borders of Canaan. As slaves, they have had their human dignity disgraced and their identity as Abraham's descendants dishonored and practically erased. But during their time in the desert, Moses receives from God a set of laws that will restore their human dignity and unique identity.

Among these laws are our final two Abrahamic practices. Sabbath, the sixth practice, sets apart the seventh day as a day of rest. Slaves, of course, have no days off; they are only given value for their service to the empire and emperor. Yet through the Sabbath, God is revealed to be no hard taskmaster or cruel slave driver; God gives you a break. In God's kingdom, there is a rhythm of work and rest for everyone. People don't live to work, but work and rest are part of life under God.

Not only does the regular rhythm of work habitually include a day of rest, but the regular rhythm of seasons is enriched with special holidays and seasons during which the past is remembered and feasts are celebrated. These special holidays give rise to various liturgical calendars that suggest we should mark our days not only with the cycles of the moon and seasons, but also with occasions to tell our children the stories of our faith community's past so that this past will have a future, and so that our ancient way and its practices will be rediscovered and renewed every year.

Pilgrimage, fasting, sacred meal, common prayer, giving, Sabbath, and liturgical year—these ancient practices have formed people of Abrahamic faith through many centuries. In so doing, they have played a key role in forming humanity. Their impact becomes all the more significant in light of the practices they in some ways counter. For example, pilgrimage leads us to cross boundaries and thus undercuts nativism, nationalism, ethnocentrism, and racism. Fasting requires self-control and so defies the self-indulgence of gluttony, lust, and greed. Both pilgrimage and fasting help us to appreciate precious, mundane things we so easily take for granted—a sandwich, a mug of hot chocolate, our own beds, our front doors or gardens.

> IN GOD'S KINGDOM, THERE IS A RHYTHM OF WORK AND REST FOR EVERYONE, AND PEOPLE DON'T LIVE TO WORK, BUT RATHER WORK AND REST ARE PART OF LIFE UNDER GOD.

The sacred meal calls us to reconciliation with God, neighbor, and enemy and thus counters the centrifugal forces of selfishness and resentment. Common prayer counters drudgery, reminding us to know God in the affairs of daily life, infusing the so-called secular with the sacred. Giving bridges the gap between rich and poor and begins to heal the rift that expands between them. Sabbath liberates the worker from the external tyranny of exploitation and the internal tyranny of workaholism. And the liturgical year counters amnesia and apathy with memory and anticipation. The world would be a far different place today, I think you'll agree, if these practices had not enlivened the three Abrahamic faiths, which have played such remarkable roles in our common global history. And the world will be a far different place in a century, or five centuries, or fifty centuries, if these ancient practices and the way they support are allowed to go extinct. But if these spiritual practices are kept alive in us and our descendants, we may discover they contain ancient resources desperately needed in the world yet to be born.

SPIRITUAL EXERCISES

1. Ponder the significance of Abraham as the patriarch of our planet's three great monotheistic faiths. Think of (or find) a friend of the other two Abrahamic faiths. Seek them out. Tell them about this chapter, and ask them about the role and significance of Abraham in their faith. Don't argue. Simply listen, learn, and seek to build common ground based on this shared source of inspiration.

2. Go over the seven Abrahamic practices and notice how the author derives them from the biblical story. Then reflect on your experiences with each of these practices. If you're in a group, share your experiences with one or two of the practices that have most touched your life. And share your questions and curiosity about the practices you have had the least experience with.

3. Consider this: your life is improved and enriched by the fact that some people are practicing dimensions of the spiritual life that you don't practice, and their lives are enriched by your practices. For example, what benefit do you derive from people who are

more dedicated to the Sabbath than you are? How might this be true of other practices?

4. Imagine the world in one thousand years, in the thirty-first century, following two scenarios: one in which the seven ancient spiritual practices have been forgotten for a thousand years, and one in which they have been revitalized and followed.

5. Reflect on your previous four answers. Let each reflection turn into a prayer that you write or speak aloud.

CHAPTER 4

PRACTICING THE WAY OF JESUS

I am a follower of Jesus. My spiritual formation has taken place in a Christian context. That's not to say I haven't learned from and been inspired by Jews, Muslims, Buddhists, Hindus, Native Peoples, atheists, and others. But it is to say (in the language of Anne Lamott) that I am at heart a Jesus-y person, and my view of God and spiritual practices has most deeply been formed in the context of the life, message, and mission of this Galilean Jew, who is seen by many Jews and all Muslims as a great man and a uniquely great prophet, and confessed by Christians to be the Savior of the world.

One cannot say his name these days without pause. Just yesterday, I was at a conference in Melbourne, Australia. Among the twenty or so people with whom I had personal conversations after my public presentations were two women who coincidentally said almost the same thing: "Whenever I hear the name Jesus, I cringe." They both told me they admired the Jesus portrayed in the Gospels, but the way Christians talked about Jesus had wounded them, embarrassed them, and made them withdraw from identifying themselves as Christians. The name of Jesus seems to be used, they said, as a kind of club with which to intimidate believers and nonbelievers, or as a kind of membership card by which some are included in a different kind of club—the Christian club. "Jesus" becomes the password that gets them access, regardless of their character, while others are excluded, equally regardless of character. One of the women began crying when she told me this, revealing an intensity of pain I have seen too often, including in the mirror. Millions of Jews, Muslims, atheists, gay and lesbian people, and others know this pain too well. When I say I am a Christ-centered person, I hope I do not evoke this kind of intimidation and exclusion, but rather the opposite.

I was talking to a Jewish friend of mine a couple of years ago about the person in question. "What do you think of Jesus?" I asked, feeling that our friendship had progressed to the point where a question like this was not only safe but welcome. "You might be surprised to know," she replied, "that many of the Jews I know think Jesus was from God, that he was a true prophet, and that our ancestors were wrong to reject him." But then she added, with more than a little irony, "But after two thousand years of anti-Semitism, you can't expect us to be too excited about the doctrine of the Trinity or the virgin birth."

I had a similar experience with another Jewish friend, who asked me, "What's the big deal about Jesus to you Christians? I just don't get it." I did my best to answer him, speaking of Jesus in the context of the Jewish people under Roman occupation, with his message of the kingdom of God and his call to a new way of life first for his fellow Jews and then for all peoples. I knew that my friend was an agnostic, even though he was very committed to practicing Judaism, so I tried to emphasize Jesus' role in relation to the Judaism he loved and in which he found meaning and life. I referred him to the call of Abraham in Genesis 12, which we considered in the previous chapter, and in particular to God telling Abraham that his descendants will become a great nation and will be blessed so they can be a blessing to all other nations. My friend was, of course, more familiar with this passage than I.

"I understand Jesus," I ended by saying, "to be the one God chose to open up the doors to Gentiles like me, to bring blessing to all nations. You might think of Jesus as the global marketing department for the God of Abraham, Isaac, and Jacob. He says, 'It's time to welcome people of every ethnic group and religion to know the one true and living God we Jews have been getting to know for centuries.'" We talked a bit more, and then my friend said good-bye. As he left, he told me, "Thanks. This conversation helped me. You know, if I believed in God, I think I could believe in that Jesus."

I've received a less enthusiastic response from some of my fellow Christians when I've talked about Jesus in these terms. I never in any way minimize the classical (and I believe profoundly true) ways of speaking of Jesus in the ancient creeds. I affirm, wholeheartedly and humbly, the mystery of the Trinity and the incarnation, Jesus' role as Savior and Lord and head of the church, the affirmations of the ancient creeds. What's gotten me into trouble, though, is my suspicion that a person can be a follower of the way of Jesus without affiliating with the Christian religion, and my simultaneous lament that a person can be accepted and even celebrated as a card-carrying member of the Christian club but not actually be a follower of the way of Jesus. And even worse, I've proposed that I would rather be a follower of the way of Jesus and not be affiliated with the Christian religion than the reverse. (Of course, I, with all my faults, am very honored to be affiliated with a wonderful religion that condescends to include sinners such as myself, expressing the grace of God in Jesus Christ. I am also grateful to be affiliated with a religion that has made so many tragic mistakes through history, as this is humbling to have to admit, and humility is good for one's education, not to mention one's soul.)

I am convinced that Jesus didn't come to start a new religion; he came to proclaim a new kingdom. He wouldn't have been killed simply for starting a new religion, because the Roman Empire was very tolerant of religions. What they were completely intolerant of, though, was the proclamation of a competing authority structure that superseded the one centered in Caesar in Rome. They reserved a special form of public torture and execution for people who dared to challenge the authority structure that brought to the Mediterranean world the *pax Romana*: the brutal semiotics of the cross.

> JESUS DIDN'T COME TO START A NEW RELIGION; HE CAME TO PROCLAIM A NEW KINGDOM.

Jesus wasn't a Christian, at least not in the sense we use the word today. He was from birth to death (and, I believe, to resurrection) a Jew. But he was a Jew who proclaimed a new way that was good news for Gentiles as well as Jews. He described this way using a number of powerful metaphors. Most evocative and important was the metaphor of the *kingdom of God*, which I've written about extensively elsewhere.[1]

By a new kingdom, Jesus meant a new way of life, a new arrangement and set of values, a new order and a new array of priorities and commitments, a new vision of peace and how to achieve it. It was, in short, a new *way* that called for new practices. For example, instead of the practice of loving friends and hating enemies, this new way called people to practice loving enemies as if they were friends. Instead of hungering and thirsting for good food and drink, it called them to practice hungering and thirsting for justice. Instead of focusing people's attention on fashion and styles of clothing, it focused people's attention on gratitude for the simple gifts of life. Instead of accommodating to the common male desire to use females and discard them, it called each man either to celibacy or to loving marital fidelity in thought as well as action.

Jesus also described this way of life as a yoke and a road. The first image evokes a young ox harnessed next to an experienced, older ox. The young animal would learn to pull the plow or cart in rhythm with his mentor and model. And by the metaphor of a road or path, Jesus didn't imply a broad and smooth Roman highway, but a twisty, rocky mountain footpath that required careful attention and commitment, step by step. One learned the path by following Jesus, by trusting him enough to imitate his example and put his words into practice. Jesus didn't merely describe this way or path, nor did he merely point to it, nor did he reduce it to a list of rules; he actually embodied it: *I am the path*, he said. *Love as I have loved. I have given you an example that you should follow.*[2]

This is exactly the language of a *way*, which Dr. Senge used in the satellite interview I described earlier. Jesus was, first and foremost, a leader gathering followers, a mentor gathering learners, a teacher gathering students, a master artist gathering apprentices, a rabbi making disciples. The process began by calling common people to an uncommon life. To fishermen, he said, "Follow me and you will start catching people instead of fish" (Matthew 4:19). To those wearied by an oppressive system—a kind of socioeconomic and spiritual pile-on that began with the Romans and then was joined by the religious establishment—he said, "Come to me and I will give you rest" (Matthew 11:28). To a member of the rich elite, he said, "Come, follow me in helping the poor" (Matthew 19:21).

Once gathered, the disciples had the opportunity, as Mark says (3:14), to "be with him" day after day as Jesus set an example of walking in this new way, as he taught this way of seeing and articulated this way of living, as he formed a community of friends. And eventually, he would send this circle of friends out to do for others exactly what he had done for them, as recorded variously in the Gospels and echoed by Paul (Matthew 28:18–20; 2 Timothy 2:2).

The phrase used by the apostle Matthew—*make disciples*—may be a bit off-putting. *Make* might evoke coercion or a kind of industrial process. But disciples are not *made* the way one makes a product: put raw material on a conveyor belt, subject it to a production line of "programs," and then let the finished product drop off the conveyor belt into a bin to be warehoused and shipped to its final destination. A better word than *make* would be *form*; disciples are formed as an artist forms a work of art—or better, disciples are formed as an artist himself is formed. The master artist sees potential in a young artist. She invites the protégé to be one of her students. There are private lessons and group lessons. A relationship develops between master and apprentice and between apprentices. Eventually the master deems the apprentice ready for a master recital or art show or debut performance, after which the apprentice is no longer an apprentice but a master him- or herself.

> JESUS NEVER MAKES "CHRISTIANS" OR "CONVERTS," BUT HE CALLS DISCIPLES AND SENDS THEM OUT TO CONTINUE THE PROCESS.

Invited or called to learn (as a disciple or art student) and then sent or commissioned to play and teach (as an apostle or master artist)—this is the pattern of Jesus' interaction with people. Discipleship and apostleship are two sides of the same coin. Jesus never makes "Christians" or "converts," but he calls disciples and sends them out to continue the process: *learn the way so you can model and teach the way to others who will do the same.*[3] The term *Christian*, by the way, occurs only 3 times in the New Testament, while the term *disciple* occurs more than 250 times.

Since we're mentioning statistics, let me add this: the Greek word *akolouzein*, which means "to follow," appears about 90 times in the New Testament, almost always related to following Jesus. Specifically, we find it 25 times in Matthew, 18 times in Mark, 17 times in Luke, and 19 times in John. This consistency (even across the "divide" between the three Synoptics and John) tells us how important this idea of following a way was to the early disciples.[4]

This may explain why many of us, if forced to choose, would rather be known primarily as Christ-followers than as adherents to the Christian religion, and it explains why to us the "Jesus thing" should probably be seen less as a religious institution and more as a movement (after all, this is what followers do: they *move* in the direction of their leader). The same might be said for the Abraham thing and the Moses thing and the Muhammad thing: they weren't intended to be static repositories of dogma or lists of

WHAT WOULD HAPPEN IF WE WERE WILLING TO RISK EVERYTHING SO THAT PEOPLE COULD BE . . . FORMED AND TRANSFORMED BY SPIRITUAL PRACTICES?

rules and rituals; they were intended to be movements, each a distinct way of living intended to bring God's shalom or *salaam* into the world.

I wonder what would happen if people today were to rediscover their religions in this light. Moreover, I wonder what would happen if we were willing to risk everything so that people could be not just indoctrinated and informed by dogmatic abstractions and ritual observances, but formed and transformed by spiritual practices, people who learn a way of life so they can move together in movements of peace, shalom, salaam?

When we commit to this understanding of faith, we will find a surprising ally: the apostle Paul.

SPIRITUAL EXERCISES

1. To what degree would you describe yourself as a "Jesus-y" person? What is the story behind your answer?
2. Reflect on three important metaphors used by Jesus: kingdom, yoke, and path. Talk about them in your own words. Explore what they evoke for you, what they challenge you to be and do, and how they speak to you in your life situation today.
3. The author contrasts Christianity as an institution on the one hand with being disciples and being part of a movement on the other. How do you respond to this contrast? What do you think would happen if the institutions of Christianity became more focused on forming disciples and supporting a movement?
4. As an experiment, try avoiding the words *Christian* and *Christianity* for the next week or month or year (your choice). Instead, use the terms *follower* (or *disciple*) *of Christ* and *the movement Jesus started.*

How would this change in terminology affect you? What problems would it cause? What insights might it produce?

5. Talk to God about Jesus, your feelings about him, your beliefs and questions, your commitment, your appreciation.

C H A P T E R   5

Poor Paul. First his critics painted him as a sinister spiritual villain who clipped the wings of the fledgling movement launched by Jesus. Then many of his self-confessed supporters hijacked his epistles (or quotes extracted from them) for their own theological projects, which range from sublime to sad.

A whole range of Pauline misreadings can quite easily be remedied, I believe, once we make a simple but profound adjustment in our approach to his work: instead of reading Jesus primarily in the light of Paul, we need to read Paul primarily in the light of Jesus. Our conventional line of sight goes back through modern preachers to Wesley or Calvin to Luther (if one is Protestant), or back through Aquinas to Augustine (if one is Catholic), or back to Basil and Gregory and Chrysostom (if one is Eastern Orthodox), penultimately to Paul, and then finally to Jesus. But the biblical narrative is better served by a line of sight starting with Abraham and proceeding through Moses to David, and then to the prophets, and then to Jesus, and then to Paul, and so on. From this perspective we can see the biblical story building to a climax in Jesus' message of the kingdom of God (or yoke of God or path of God). Then we can see Paul's message echoing Jesus' message, calling people to a way of life characterized by reconciliation with God, one another, and all creation in a global community.

If we try to see the story unfold in this way, flowing from Jesus to Paul, the plot takes an unexpected turn in the months and years after Jesus' departure. To nearly everyone's surprise, it becomes clear that the way of God taught by Jesus will include Gentiles as well as Jews. This is no small adjustment. After all, how can bacon-eating, Sabbath-breaking, uncircumcised newbies be equals and partners in the mission of God in the world with people who are part of a two-thousand-year-old sacred tradition? How can this radical inclusiveness be justified in terms of the Hebrew Scriptures? How can it be worked out practically in faith communities spread across the Roman Empire?

INSTEAD OF READING JESUS PRIMARILY IN THE LIGHT OF PAUL, WE NEED TO READ PAUL PRIMARILY IN THE LIGHT OF JESUS.

This is precisely where Paul steps in. As a former Pharisee and bitter enemy of the Jesus way, he knows what this fledgling movement has to overcome in order to be more inclusive. Perhaps because of his background, he sees as nobody else can how precious and needed—and fragile and vulnerable—the reconciling way of Jesus is. Paul the Pharisee becomes Paul the apostle to the Gentiles.

He focuses his formidable intellect and indefatigable energy on forging the nascent fellowship of Jesus into a truly multicultural community, one body composed of Jews and Gentiles, male and female, slave and free, educated and uneducated.

He pursues his mission in many ways. In person and via his writings, Paul uses the Jewish Scriptures to defend and legitimize this unimagined and unprecedented innovation of Gentile inclusion. He travels tirelessly with a diversified team, seeking to model the way of reconciliation initiated by Jesus' message of the kingdom of God. He takes a financial collection from Gentiles, which will be given to poor and suffering Jews, building their mutual affection and indebtedness. He confronts passionately—at times vehemently—anyone who seeks to divide asunder the diverse community that God has joined together in Christ. Paul's goal is not to define a gospel different from Jesus' gospel of the kingdom or yoke or pathway of God, but to grapple with a monumental challenge of living and working out

THEN WE CAN SEE PAUL'S MESSAGE ECHOING JESUS' MESSAGE, CALLING PEOPLE TO A WAY OF LIFE CHARACTERIZED BY RECONCILIATION WITH GOD, ONE ANOTHER, AND ALL CREATION IN A GLOBAL COMMUNITY.

that message as it embraces, against all odds, Jews and non-Jews, men and women, slaves and free, vegetarians and meat eaters, the scrupulously religious and the spiritual-but-not-religious, the conventional and the unconventional.

Take, for example, Paul's epistle to the Romans, and read it from beginning to end, focusing on the document's main theme: "to the Jew first and also to the Greek" (1:16 NRSV). Paul begins by "tricking" his Jewish readers into judging their Gentile neighbors, but then he reminds them that they are no better. After proving that "all have sinned"—the religious Jew as well as the irreligious Gentile—he says that God's grace in Christ flows to all (3:23). He makes the point again and again, coming from one angle and then another, taking up one metaphor after

> **PAUL, LIKE JESUS, IS A LOVE GUY, CALLING PEOPLE TO FOLLOW A LOVE ROAD, TO WALK A LOVE PATH, TO PRACTICE A LOVE WAY.**

another. Then he addresses specific issues—arcane and culturally odd to us—regarding eating meat sacrificed to idols, the observance of holy days, and so on, calling both Jew and Gentile not to judge one another, but to love one another "without hypocrisy" and to "accept one another" without "disputations" (12:9; 15:7; 14:1).

The letter ends with an extensive description of a "way" (15:28), along with exhortations regarding specific practices for followers of the way. In nearly all his primary letters (including Galatians, Ephesians, and Colossians), Paul follows the same pattern—reflections on the gospel's inclusiveness of Jew and Gentile, and then descriptions of a common way of life to which all are called, with exhortations to practice it in very concrete ways.[1]

In his first letter to the church in Corinth, where the cultural conflicts and divisions are especially intense, Paul's teaching is equally so, climaxing in a chapter that is too often trivialized as a wedding poem: 1 Corinthians 13. "I will show you a more excellent way," Paul promises (12:31 NRSV), and then he describes "the way of love." He concludes, "Follow the way of love" (14:1 TNIV). Without love, he says, nothing else matters at all, a conclusion he echoes in Galatians with equally strong language: "The only thing that counts is faith expressing itself through love" (Galatians 5:6). Far from being a rigid member of the dogma police or inquisition mafia, Paul, like Jesus, is a prophet of love, calling people to follow a love road, to walk a love path, to practice a love way. Paul's faith is not just an idea to which we assent but a way in which we walk. Contemporary translations tend to obscure rather than reveal Paul's pervasive and poetic use of way-walking imagery. Consider a few samples from the more than two dozen times Paul uses this language:

> " . . . so we too might walk in newness of life." (Romans 6:4 NASB)
> " . . . who do not walk according to the flesh but according to the Spirit." (Romans 8:4 NRSV)
> " . . . you are no longer walking according to love." (Romans 14:15 NASB)
> " . . . we walk by faith, not by sight." (2 Corinthians 5:7 NRSV)
> " . . . walk by the Spirit." (Galatians 5:16)
> " . . . walk in [good works]." (Ephesians 2:10, paraphrased)
> " . . . walk in . . . love." (Ephesians 5:2 TNIV)
> " . . . walk in a manner worthy of the Lord." (Colossians 1:10 NASB)

" . . . as you have received Christ Jesus the Lord, so walk in him." (Colossians 2:6)

Interestingly, Paul associates the process of learning this way of life with the practices of physical exercise.

> Do you not know that in a race all the runners run, but only one gets the prize? Run in such a way as to get the prize. Everyone who competes in the games goes into strict training. They do it to get a crown that will not last; but we do it to get a crown that will last forever. Therefore I do not run like someone running aimlessly; I do not fight like a boxer beating the air. No, I strike a blow to my body and make it my slave so that after I have preached to others, I myself will not be disqualified for the prize. (1 Corinthians 9:24–27 TNIV)

Paul employs similar exercise imagery in his first epistle to Timothy:

> Train yourself in godliness, for, while physical training is of some value, godliness is valuable in every way, holding promise for both the present life and the life to come. (1 Timothy 4:8 NRSV)

And in Ephesians 4:20, he speaks of us "learning Christ"—as if Christ were a language or skill or art we must practice.[2] To learn a way, then, we go step-by-step; we discipline ourselves; we train ourselves through practice; we exercise our faculties as an athlete does. In so doing, we become people we previously were not, with capabilities that were previously beyond us.

Practice (or exercise) may not make perfect, but as we will see in more detail later, it does make currently impossible things *possible*.[3] The one who tries to run a marathon can't do it, but the one who trains eventually can. The one who tries to lift a heavy weight can't do it, but the one who exercises his muscles on lighter weights eventually can. The one who dreams of playing Mozart on the violin can't actually do it, but the one who practices—doing various finger exercises, melodic warm-ups, bowing drills, and so on—eventually can. And the one who wants to be patient, kind, forgiving, courageous, just, joyful, peaceful, and resilient can never do it; the harder she tries, the more frustrated she will become. But the one who trains and exercises herself becomes what she was incapable of being before.

Yet this is not the whole picture. For Paul, personal exertion or exercise is necessary but not sufficient. Without exercise or practice we will not experience transformation, but neither can we produce it through exercise and practice alone. There is another empowerment, utterly indispensable, variously identified as the power of God, the grace of God, and the Holy Spirit:

- "Work out your salvation with fear and trembling, for it is God who works in you both to will and act according to his good purpose." (Philippians 2:12–13)
- "But by the grace of God I am what I am, and his grace to me was not without effect. No, I worked harder than all of them—yet not I, but the grace of God that was with me." (1 Corinthians 15:10)
- "So I say, live by the Spirit, and you will not gratify the desires of the sinful nature." (Galatians 5:16)

Paul so intertwines human exertion with divine energy that it's hard to tell where his strength ends and God's strength begins: "To this end I labor, struggling with all his energy, which so powerfully works in me" (Colossians 1:29). We can go further and say it is impossible for Paul to distinguish where his life ends and God's life in him begins: "I have been crucified with Christ and I no longer live, but Christ lives in me. The life I live in the body, I live by faith in the Son of God who loved me and gave himself for me" (Galatians 2:20).

Paul's use of pregnancy imagery dramatically captures the inseparable intercourse of human and divine power: "My dear children, for whom I am again in the pains of childbirth until Christ is formed in you" (Galatians 4:19). Although Paul frequently mixes and twists metaphors (*he* experiences labor pains so *they* can be pregnant with Christ), the image still conveys the unique synergy of pregnancy. Pregnancy requires a woman to receive what only a man can bring to her. Yet the new life that grows within her couldn't have been produced by the man alone; it is very literally part of her, requiring her to carry it and, through labor, to give birth to it. (The Eastern Orthodox celebration of Mary as *theotokos* celebrates this synergy of Mary and the Holy Spirit.) So for Paul, as we receive the Holy Spirit, as we receive grace and empowerment, Christ is formed within us, and we give birth to him in the world. Later in Galatians, Paul uses parallel imagery: the seed of Christ has been planted in us, and if we tend the seed (in another mixed metaphor, by "walking in the Spirit"), we will bear the fruit of the Spirit in the world (5:22).[4]

> **IT'S NOT SIMPLY A DOCTRINE OR TEACHING THAT PAUL WANTS TO CONVEY; IT'S A WAY OF LIFE THAT'S SEEN AS WELL AS HEARD.**

Paul doesn't simply teach the way of love and call people to learn Christ through words alone, however. He is acutely aware of the necessity of modeling through example this way of life (Acts 20:18–20, 31, 33–35; 1 Corinthians 11:1; 1 Thessalonians 1:6, 2:6–12). Paul wants to convey not simply a doctrine or teaching, but a way of life that's seen as well as heard: "Whatever you have learned or received or heard from me, or seen in me—put it into practice" (Philippians 4:9).

We can hear Paul's authentic voice only in profound continuity with Jesus, embedded in the biblical narrative that climaxes in Jesus. We can recognize him as a fellow human being like us, frail and weak (as he himself confessed on many occasions), easily misunderstood (as his colleague Peter acknowledged), but risking all to follow and lead others in the new way of Jesus, a way he himself opposed until it won his heart and changed his direction.

SPIRITUAL EXERCISES

1. What is your impression of Paul? Do you see him as someone who changed the course of the early Christian movement so that it departed from Jesus' way and example, or as someone who followed in Jesus' way and expanded it?
2. Review Paul's use of walking imagery. How does it affect, inspire, or encourage you? Today, as you are physically walking, try to recall this imagery and let the idea of walking in the Spirit work on your imagination.
3. Review Paul's use of pregnancy imagery. How does it reveal the spiritual life as a "way"? What does this imagery suggest about the role of the Holy Spirit, the grace of God, and the power of God at work within us?
4. Think of your spiritual life as a "way of love," and read 1 Corinthians 13 each day for the next week, month, or year (your

choice). Learn 1 Corinthians 13 "by heart" and see what effect it has on you.

5. Use any or all of the passages from Paul's writings mentioned in this chapter as a basis for a written or spoken prayer.

CHAPTER 6

SHARING TREASURES AMONG FRIENDS

The story of the Christian faith, like that of Judaism and Islam, can be seen as the story of a community given a way, then drifting off course, then finding its way again, then losing it again, recovering it, and so on. Two steps forward, one step back, a detour to the left, a lurch to the right, wandering, slipping, falling, rising again. The journey isn't easy, and we never arrive. But the way—Jewish *torah*, Christian gospel, or Muslim *deen*—leads us toward the peace, wisdom, and joy we seek. If we stop pursuing it, we will be stuck where we are.

One of our most common temptations is to turn the way into a place, to turn the adventure into a status, to trade the runway for the hangar, to turn the holy path into a sitting room—even if we call it a sanctuary. When the movement becomes an institution, those whose hearts call them to pilgrimage get restless. For example, when the previously persecuted church became socially acceptable in the fourth century, when a person was considered a Christian simply for being born in the Roman Empire, many people seeking the way left the comfort of Empire and made their way to the desert for a greater challenge. In the desert wastelands, the monastic way of life took shape under the guidance of the desert fathers and mothers.

Similarly on the margins of the Roman Empire, the Celtic Christian community emerged.

Nevertheless, whenever the practice of the Christian way lapsed into stagnancy, a new leader would arise among them and call the people from complacency to a more radical way of life. By the thirteenth century, even the monastic movements had in many cases slowed to a standstill, hardening their categories and losing their momentum. Then Catholic reformers like Saint Francis burst on the scene with a song and a smile, revitalizing the monastic life and bringing to the church a fresh vision of faith as a way.

WHEN THE MOVEMENT BECOMES AN INSTITUTION, THOSE WHOSE HEART CALL THEM TO PILGRIMAGE GET RESTLESS.

Martin Luther, the Anabaptists, the Pietists, the Great Awakenings, the Wesleys, the Social Gospelers, the Pentecostals, the charismatics, the Latin American base communities, and many others have represented successive waves of renewal, stirring the pot in various ways, shaking the status quo, waking the slumbering, reminding the faithful that they were called not to a comfortable seat in a well-appointed waiting room but to a steep and winding footpath toward a life that is truly alive.

Sometimes the church has tried to codify or institutionalize the way: *attend the required Sunday and holiday services, participate in the expected rituals or programs, don't dispute with church teaching or authority, and all will be well.* But time and again, the equation has been confirmed: institutional participation + 0 = nominalism and stagnation. In recent centuries the church has tried to improve the equation with programs for Christian education and discipleship. Helpful as such efforts have been, they have often reinforced the mistaken idea that more knowledge leads to better behavior In other words, *knowledge=growth*.

This knowledge-acquisition approach in some cases supplemented and in others supplanted the institutional-participation approach. For many people, the quest for knowledge leads to spiritual vitality and lifelong learning, but for others it is a temptation to know-it-all judgmentalism or apathetic and rigid dogmatism. Recognizing this danger, the holiness, Pentecostal, and charismatic movements replaced or augmented the quest for knowledge with a quest for experience. They developed camp meetings, revivals, and other opportunities for faith to be more deeply felt and more thoroughly understood.

In these warmhearted

FROM THE SEVENTEENTH TO THE TWENTIETH CENTURIES, ASTUTE LEADERS SOUGHT TO EXTEND THE VISION OF THE CHRISTIAN LIFE BEYOND MERE INSTITUTIONAL PARTICIPATION.

communities, the more frequently and intensely one is touched by the Holy Spirit—often evidenced by speaking in tongues, shedding tears, shouting or dancing or being "slain in the Spirit," and so on—the better off one will be, yielding a new formula: *spiritual experiences = growth*. By the mid-twentieth century, many individuals and churches hybridized one or more of these approaches, creating what is probably the dominant formula in vital churches today: *institutional participation + knowledge + spiritual experiences = growth.*

More recently, some degree of disillusionment has set in with the newer knowledge-acquisition and experience-acquisition approaches, just as it did with the older institutional-participation approach. This disillusionment is perpetuated by the religious-consumer mentality, which keeps the faithful shopping for the latest, greatest seminar, teaching series, conference, concert, or revival.

A MORE HOLISTIC AND INTEGRAL CONCEPT OF SPIRITUAL FORMATION HAS BEGUN TO EMERGE.

In recent decades a more holistic and integral concept of spiritual formation has begun to emerge. So-called "ancient-future" Christians have reached back, drawing from early church traditions: Orthodox, Catholic, Celtic, and monastic.[1] Yet they aren't simply traditionalists; they are innovators as well. They search for spiritual resources outside their parochial parameters: Baptists learning from Catholics, Mennonites learning from Greek Orthodox, Pentecostals learning from Copts. This is innovation enough. But they also seek to integrate resources from previously discrete sources: Pentecostals praying in tongues *and* using the Eastern "Jesus prayer" *and* practicing Catholic spiritual direction *and* doing evangelical-style Bible study, for example. These catholic-ancient-futurists distribute and dialogue about the resources they discover through innovative means: MP3s and downloadable videos, blogs, podcasts, Web sites, and DVDs. Inevitably, the innovators develop a kind of formula as well:

institutional participation (in churches and parachurch organizations), *knowledge* (of the Bible, theology, Christian history) + *experiences* (of the Holy Spirit, of brokenness, of community, of mission) + *relationships* (in small groups, mentoring) + *suffering* + *service* + *time* = *growth* + *health*.

But for all of its increased nuance, this kind of formula still misses the mark. To use a formula at all is misleading, because nobody understands this approach to be foolproof. Human foolishness can trump any methodology.

To guard against our tendency to turn any new insights into formulas, we can approach the Christian faith as a way of life that is learned and strengthened through a wide variety of practices developed by Christians across traditions and over centuries. Spiritual health and growth are nurtured by this heritage as we acquire knowledge, position ourselves to receive spiritual experiences, deepen spiritual relationships, face and endure suffering, and move toward others in service.

THIS WAY OF LIFE IS LEARNED AND STRENGTHENED THROUGH A WIDE VARIETY OF PRACTICES DEVELOPED BY CHRISTIANS ACROSS THE CENTURIES AND ACROSS TRADITIONS.

Again, to resist formulas, we can envision this heritage not as the meal for which we hunger, but as a list of ingredients. Eating flour, eggs, sugar, vanilla, and chocolate chips is not the same as eating fresh-baked cookies. Between the ingredients and the cookies is the process we call cooking, which consists of practices such as sifting, stirring, waiting, cooling, heating, cutting, basting, rolling, marinating, frying, and so on. We need not only the right ingredients but also the right *way*—the right cooking practices, in the right order, at the right time.

In this light, we might think of our various denominations and traditions as different schools of cooking—French, Mexican, Italian, Chinese, Indian. Within each school, there are subtraditions of specific flavors and delights; Szechuan is distinct from Hunan within Chinese cooking, and Tandoori is distinct from Hyderabadi in Indian cooking. These differences reflect the place and time in which the school developed. Over time, different schools share ingredients and practices, producing different variations on one another's specialties. Some forms of cooking—Cajun, for example, or Asian fusion—are themselves obvious mixtures of previous cooking traditions.

Perhaps the emerging spiritual formation movement can be seen as this kind of fusion. It's new, but it's old. It's working with the same ingredients and the same practices, but combining them in fresh—and some would say tasty and nourishing—ways.

My own spiritual autobiography reflects this ancient-future fusion. I grew up in a small, warmhearted, mildly fundamentalist group called the Plymouth Brethren (made famous by ex-Brethren notables such as storyteller Garrison Keillor, *Sojourners* founder Jim Wallis, and new abolitionist David Batstone). The Brethren derived their unique blend of practices from a mixture of Anglican, Quaker, and Baptist resources, although they often claim to derive solely from study of the New Testament. (Legitimizing themselves by reference to the New Testament alone rather than Christian tradition is itself a Brethren practice.) For the Brethren, Christianity went astray in the early centuries and began to be restored first in the Reformation and then more fully in the 1830s with—guess who— the founders of the Brethren.

The Brethren's unique history gives them, like every denomination or sect, a unique "cooking style" or flavor. For example, Lutherans might study the Bible in a search for themes of law and grace or a theology of glory versus a theology of the cross. Presbyterians might study it by looking for themes of covenants, election, God's sovereign grace, and human depravity. But Brethren traditionally study the Bible in terms of dispensations, periods of time during which, they believe, God worked with humanity in different ways. And when they practice the Eucharist, they do so differently than, say, Catholics or Mennonites. I grew up being taught to defend the exclusive rightness of our flavor and to look with pity (if not disdain) on the poor souls who didn't share our taste for truth.

> **VARYING SPIRITUAL PRACTICES WITH ALL OF THEIR NUANCES AND STYLES ARE BEING SHARED ACROSS TRADITIONS.**

Some are content to remain unquestioning within the flavor and style inherited from their natal community. But for others, life gets messy and less simple, and they need a way that reflects the complexities with which they see the world.

So now we have Baptists who practice the stations of the cross (© Catholic) and Catholics who speak in tongues (© Pentecostal). Pentecostals learn the Jesus Prayer (© Eastern Orthodox), and Episcopalians sometimes baptize by immersion (© Baptist). Critics see these patterns as a terrible loss and view such innovators as spiritual dilettantes. Superficial borrowing can be a danger, but so can the refusal to learn from other traditions and share one's practices with an open hand.

Had I had been forced to choose between remaining a traditional member of the Plymouth Brethren plus nothing for my whole life or dropping out of church, I would probably be a dropout today, because as grateful as I am for my heritage, it lacked breathing room. As I drifted away from my Brethren nest, I went through a few experiences of what I call a "lateral conversion," meaning I became a card-carrying charismatic for a while and then a card-carrying Calvinist for a while, and then an amalgam of both, holding to each tradition's practices with the same proprietary zeal with which the Brethren had taught me to hold to Brethrenism, with no learning or borrowing from others. Eventually, I felt the same claustrophobia in my new traditions, so instead of converting to yet another tradition to which I would adhere in the same way I adhered to my original tradition, I converted to a different way of holding traditions in general.

I think that's part of what's going on in this time of change and transition. Old sectarian turf wars are giving way to a sharing of resources—heroes, practices, flavors, and styles of practice. And this, in a way, is itself a new practice, namely, the sharing of previously proprietary practices. We might say that Christianity is beginning to go "open source."

SPIRITUAL EXERCISES

1. The author contrasts the sanctuary (as sitting room or waiting room) with the path/ road on which one is active, on the move. To what degree do you see your faith as a sitting and waiting faith in contrast to a walking and on-the-road faith?

2. Review the institutional-participation, knowledge-acquisition, and experience-acquisition approaches, and reflect on the impact of each on your life.

3. Think about your faith community—the church, denomination, or movement of which you are part—in light of the metaphor of a tradition of cooking. How would you describe the "flavors" and "cooking practices" of your heritage? Where is it strong and delicious? Where is it otherwise?

4. Are you curious about other religious traditions? What attracts or repels you about them?

5. What experiences have you had in sharing spiritual or religious "spices," "cooking traditions," and the like?

6. Keeping this cooking metaphor in mind, what are you hungry for? Where do you feel underfed or overfed or malnourished? Turn this hunger into a prayer.

CHAPTER 7

OPEN-SOURCE SPIRITUALITY

My high school friends Scott and Paul were Baptists, Mary Lou a
Catholic charismatic, Gail a Catholic noncharismatic, and Larry a
Baptist turned Pentecostal. As friends who followed Jesus, we naturally shared our practices and
learned from one another.
Because of Larry, all of us
raised our hands when we
sang certain worship songs.
Because of Mary Lou and
Gail, we guys dropped at
least some of our anti-
Catholic prejudices. Because
of Scott and Paul, we learned
to testify and evangelize like
Baptists. Because of me, we
held open meetings, where
anybody could lead out in prayer or a reflection on the Bible—a
treasure from my Brethren heritage.

APPRENTICESHIP IS ONE OF THE KEY WAYS THAT SPIRITUAL FORMATION HAPPENS.

We were all peer mentors to one another, simultaneously

apprentices and teachers, giving one another access to the heroes and practices and theologies of our varying traditions.

The spiritual life is less science than art, and like any art, it is learned through apprenticeship. Through apprenticeship, our lives become open sources of embodied practices for one another.

THE SPIRITUAL LIFE IS LESS SCIENCE THAN ART, AND LIKE ANY ART, IT IS LEARNED THROUGH APPRENTICESHIP.

I feel unspeakably fortunate in this regard. Throughout my Christian life, I've had an amazing set of mentors: close friends and those who have mentored me from afar through their books. Early on, Dave invited me to a Bible study, and from him I learned the practice of immersing myself in a passage or book of the Bible—Romans 12 and 1 Corinthians 13, and then the book of 1 Thessalonians. He also taught me the beautiful practice of having a daily quiet time, for many evangelicals the essential spiritual practice; for Catholics, like praying the rosary; or for Eastern Orthodox believers, like praying the Jesus Prayer.

Rod taught me the practice of hanging out, simply being with people so we could draw out the best in one another. This included associating with people whom others rejected, realizing that broken, addicted, dysfunctional, and hard-to-love people were important to God and should be to me as well.

There were two more Daves. The second Dave taught me to read through entire sections of the Bible so that I could get a sense of the whole in order to make sense of the parts. The third Dave mentored me in the practice of preaching, how to work responsibly with a biblical text and open it up for people. Although he can't be blamed for all the people I have bored in my talks and sermons, he can be credited for everyone I have in some small way encouraged, instructed, or inspired.

Tom didn't use the words *confession* or *spiritual direction,* but he created safe space for me to admit my sins and weaknesses and fears and doubts, and he introduced me to a depth of spiritual friendship I had never experienced. (He also taught me to drink an occasional beer, which was a certain kind of spiritual breakthrough for a boy raised fundamentalist, but that's another story.) Once, Tom told me about a book called *Practicing the Presence of God* by a medieval monk named Brother Lawrence. I'd never heard of this practice before, but from the day he told me about it, I began doing it, and it has been one of the most important practices of my spiritual life. Once Tom bought me a journal and told me how helpful it had been for him to start writing down his prayers. "It keeps your mind from wandering and running laps without getting anywhere when you pray," he said. I'd never heard of the practice of journaling before, but with his coaching and encouragement, it too became a mainstay of my spiritual formation.

I will be forever grateful to Rennie for introducing me to the majesty and beauty of the Book of Common Prayer. I had never before used "common prayers" or collects (pronounced *co*-lects, prayers that are read together), and when Rennie led in the reading of a collect, he did it with such joy and enthusiasm that all who joined him were caught up in its beauty and meaning. And years later, Phyllis introduced me to the practice of taking those prayers into my private life and inserting them into my day at certain fixed hours. What I learned from her books became even more alive one day when we were talking and she looked at her watch and said, "It's time to pray. Would you like to pray with me?" She pulled out a little prayer book—exactly the same one I had been using, I noticed—and together we refreshed our souls in the awareness of God's presence. Stan taught me a practice necessary for anyone with a public life: how to receive and respond to criticism graciously. He did this—not by criticizing me—but by modeling a gracious response to his own critics, many of whom I inherited after his untimely death. It's hard to stop recounting stories like this, because the most important things I've learned have come through a person who modeled a practice and then explained it to me, encouraged me to try it, and sometimes checked in later to see how I was doing with it.

> **THE MOST IMPORTANT THINGS I'VE LEARNED HAVE COME THROUGH A PERSON WHO MODELED A PRACTICE AND THEN EXPLAINED IT TO ME, ENCOURAGED ME TO TRY IT, AND SOMETIMES CHECKED IN LATER TO SEE HOW I WAS DOING.**

Just last year, I traveled with Rene Padilla. I was fifty, he about seventy-five, and I saw in him the practice of living from a quiet center. Over several weeks on the road together, I marveled at his strength and serenity as he poured himself out, rested, and poured himself out again. The age difference between Rene and me is, I think, significant. We can learn from people of any age—peers or younger—but I've noticed that a twenty- or twenty-five-year gap in age seems to be ideal for mentoring and apprenticeship. One is farther down the road, but not so far

as to have forgotten what it was like to be younger. Some people—
and I pray I will be one of them—never forget what it was like, which
enables them to mentor people of any age.

My experience, perhaps, is unusual—to have had so many
excellent mentors who embodied such a rich array of practices from
so many traditions and made themselves an open source to me.

The term *open source* draws from the world of technology,
where, in 1998, some software developers in Palo Alto, California,
instead of keeping their codes secret as proprietary information
under their control, offered them to the general public and invited
willing volunteers to participate in their ongoing development and
adaptation. A similar process (using the term *request for comments*
instead of *open source*) was used to develop the Internet in the late
1960s, and open-source methodology has played an expanding role
in the development of the Internet in the years since, especially in
projects like Wikipedia and YouTube.

As more and more of us open our lives to be sources of inspiration and examples for one another, we begin to seize the unfulfilled
promise of the Reformation with its open-source concept of *the priesthood of all believers*. Similar concepts were affirmed in Vatican II.[1] It's
true that not everyone can go to seminary. Not everyone can go live
in a monastery. But all of us can wake up to the people around us,
whose lives embody—not perfectly, but authentically—practices of
the spiritual life. And each of us can aspire to become an open source
of embodied spiritual practices for the benefit of others.

SPIRITUAL EXERCISES

1. List some of the spiritual mentors from your past: a pastor, a youth
   leader, a camp counselor, a relative. Call them or write them a note

or e-mail to thank them specifically for what you saw in them and learned from them. Maybe send them a gift as an expression of your love and affection. Thank God for them as well.

2. Think of peers with whom you share a peer mentorship now. Try to put into words for them what they mean in your life. Thank God for them.

3. Think of some people younger or less experienced than you in the way of Christ. Ask God to help you be an open source of encouragement and an example for them. Pray for them.

4. Try this thought experiment: imagine that all pastors, theologians, ministers, priests, and other religious professionals were required to get a "regular job." Imagine that all church services were shut down and church buildings closed, all denominations disbanded. Imagine that the only way Christian faith could survive was through people living it and passing it on to others through friendship and daily informal interaction. What outcomes can you imagine from this situation? What can you learn from this thought experiment?

CHAPTER 8

SHALLOW TROUBLE, DEEP TROUBLE

If you've lost your way to the desired destination, you're in shallow trouble. But if in the process you've also lost the address you were supposed to visit, your trouble just got *deep*. If you don't realize you've forgotten what your desired destination is, you're in the bottomless pit the great Dane Søren Kierkegaard called the deepest level of despair—namely, to be in a hopeless situation but not realize it or feel bad about it. Let's hope, as a reader of a book like this, even though you may be in deep trouble, your trouble is at least not of the bottomless type.

In the last decade or so, my conviction has grown that our troubles in the Christian religion are deep and, for too many of us, bottomless. Many Muslims and Jews may draw a similar conclusion about their respective communities. Recent attempts—ugly and combative at best—at atheist evangelism may even convince the atheist community that their troubles aren't shallow either.[1]

So, as we regain a sense of the profound importance of faith as a way of life, and before we consider the vital importance of practices, we also must regain a sense of the destination to which the way and practices are supposed to take us.

Traditionally, Christians have spoken of two destinations: heaven and hell. But as different as those two destinations are, they have something important in common: they are both out of this world, at least as commonly understood. So, what if we flip the conventional script about ninety degrees? Our two vertical columns of heaven and hell now become two horizontal rows, and we can divide both rows into two new columns: the afterlife, beyond history as we know it, and this life, in history as we know it.

BEFORE WE CONSIDER THE VITAL IMPORTANCE OF PRACTICES, WE ALSO MUST REGAIN A SENSE OF THE DESTINATION TO WHICH THE WAY AND PRACTICES ARE SUPPOSED TO TAKE US.

Please understand: I'm not saying anything here on my beliefs about heaven and hell; I've opened that question elsewhere.[2] I'm certainly not saying that the difference between heaven and hell is insignificant. Instead, I'm saying that both heaven and hell as popularly understood are destinations beyond history and outside of this earth. And I'm raising the question of whether focusing on the afterlife beyond history can unintentionally but tragically lead to the abandonment of this earth and this life. And I'm raising the possibility that in doing so, we find ourselves leaning our ladder on the wrong building, or choosing the wrong destination as we set out on our way, thus plunging ourselves into deep trouble and potentially, if we never give our direction and destination a second thought, bottomless trouble.

So let's call this chapter an extended thought experiment. We have two possible destinations or goals toward which to pursue our way. Assuming that nobody wants to lean his or her ladder against eternal torment in hell after this life—or for that matter, a hell on earth between now and then—one goal is heaven: a timeless, disembodied (we could say Neoplatonic) state into which we enter at death or when our space-time universe is destroyed. Harps, angels, and clouds are optional; the presence of God is essential, as is the absence of evil, pain, suffering, and sadness.

The other building upon which we can lean our ladder, or the other goal toward which we can direct our way, is God's will being done on earth as it is in heaven, the development of the kind of world God wants to see our world become. To repeat, we can lean our ladder on a building called "Escape from Earth to Be with God in Heaven," or we can lean our ladder on a different building called "Joining God in Healing This Earth from Personal and Social Evil."

The difference between these two buildings wouldn't be so significant if it weren't for this fact: the kind of person who wants to participate in the healing of the world is very different from the kind of person who wants to leave this world behind so she can go to a better one.[3] That difference deserves a bit of additional reflection.

If your goal is to produce

I'M RAISING THE QUESTION OF WHETHER FOCUSING ON THE AFTERLIFE BEYOND HISTORY CAN UNINTENTIONALLY BUT TRAGICALLY LEAD TO THE ABANDONMENT OF THIS EARTH AND THIS LIFE.

firefighters and rescue workers, you have to produce people willing to enter burning buildings. They do this not because they love fire, but because they hate it, and they despise the damage it can do to people and their dreams. Their hatred of fire and their love of safety draws them toward fire and danger. Contrast this to two other kinds of people: pyromaniacs (or arsonists) and pyrophobes. Pyromaniacs love fires and the damage they cause, and so start them. Pyrophobes fear fires and avoid them at any cost.

Similarly, if your goal is to produce doctors and health care workers, you have to produce people willing to get close to disease. They do this not because they love disease, but because they hate it and they despise the damage that disease can do to people and their dreams. Their hatred of disease and their love of health draw them close to sickness, seeking to understand it in order to treat it. They aren't like a careless sex addict who has HIV and doesn't care whom he infects, nor are they like a person with OCD who is constantly driven by a fear of germs to wash her hands a hundred times a day and to avoid anyone and anything that could possibly infect her. In contrast, health care workers are willing to get up close and personal with disease, but they do so in order to fight disease and promote health.

> IF YOUR GOAL IS TO PRODUCE FIREFIGHTERS AND RESCUE WORKERS, YOU HAVE TO PRODUCE PEOPLE WILLING TO ENTER BURNING BUILDINGS.

Similarly, consider a social worker who works with violent teen offenders. She hates violence—domestic abuse, gang fights, robbery, rape. She despises what it does to people and their dreams. She devotes her life—even risks her life—for the cause of peace and to fight against violence. She isn't drawn to violence the way a gangster is, nor does she run from it like a coward might. She is drawn toward the very thing she hates in order to stop it.

My concern is that by making heaven after this life the destination of our way, we are spiritually forming people who run away from fire, disease, and the violence of our world. That's certainly a major step up from forming pyromaniacs, disease vectors, or violent delinquents. But it's not as good as what Jesus set out to do, and I think the same could be said for Moses and Muhammad. My concern is that Jesus was more like a firefighter or doctor or social worker who walks boldly into the danger in order to try to stop it.

IF A HEALED AND HEALTHY EARTH IS YOUR DESTINATION, THE WAY TO THAT GOAL PROMOTES INVOLVEMENT, ENGAGEMENT, RISK, AND PARTICIPATION.

If a healed and healthy earth is your destination, the way to that goal promotes involvement, engagement, risk, and participation. If the earth is a lost cause to you, then you will abandon this life and world for the afterlife. You will choose the way of withdrawal, isolation, self-protection, and self-distancing. By choosing one destination, you follow the way of incarnation and transformation; by choosing the other destination, you choose evacuation and abdication. Very different destinations, very different ways to them.

We now have enough centuries of history to see the way produced by the ultimate destination of hell avoidance and earth abandonment. The picture, I would say, is not entirely ugly, nor is it
entirely pretty. In the hell-avoidance context, some real saints
develop—people of deep character and godliness, people who radiate the love and spirit of Christ. But I would say they develop this
to some degree in spite of the conventional afterlife-destination system rather than because of it.[4]

What if we believe, instead, that God's goal or destination for
creation is a healed and healthy earth, with plant and animal and
human systems that share in that health? What if we believe that for
God, the earth is not a lost cause at all, but rather it's the setting in
which God's love and power will bring resurrection and liberation
and salvation? If that happens, then we can bring together two
polarities that have been, in the conventional system, in constant
tension.[5] We could picture their tension like this:

$$\longleftarrow\!\longrightarrow$$

CONTEMPLATIVE WAY   **ACTIVIST WAY**
Personal Gospel   Social Gospel
Private Piety   Common Good
Heaven-Centered   Earth-Centered
Sin-Averse   Injustice-Averse

Many of us have discovered the unsatisfying imbalance and
unsustainability of this polarity. We have watched individuals and
denominations swing—sometimes in a matter of years, sometimes
in generations—between these poles. We have learned that the contemplative way, on its own, easily becomes individualized and pri-

vatized, leading to a grotesque spiritual elitism or narcissism that is spiritual only in a debased way. The activist way, divorced from contemplation and personal piety, leads to burnout and descends into a kind of ideology that is spiritual in name only.[6]

But what happens if we realize that this is a false binary, a bad choice? What if we realize that God cares about both this life and the afterlife, that for God, who is not a dualist, they are both just different facets of one reality called *life*? What if we realize that a phrase like *kingdom of God* can be understood to encompass both? What if we put God in the center and bend both poles around God? I think this happens in phases for many of us, as we pass from duality through mutuality to harmony.

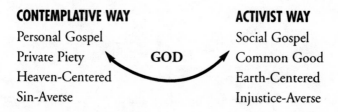

CONTEMPLATIVE WAY		ACTIVIST WAY
Personal Gospel		Social Gospel
Private Piety	**GOD**	Common Good
Heaven-Centered		Earth-Centered
Sin-Averse		Injustice-Averse

In the middle phase, which I would call *mutuality*, we become dissatisfied with the old polarity or duality. We begin seeking balance. We realize that our counterparts at the other end of the spectrum have something to teach us, and we have something to offer them. We still locate ourselves on one side or the other, but we begin seeking mutuality, mutual sharing of strengths and insights, practices and ways of living. We keep our inherited theological contracts intact, so to speak, but we add fine print to compensate for their inherent imbalance. If the process of mutuality continues, this phase will give way to another.

In this phase, which I would call harmony or maturity, earth and heaven are brought together in the life of God, and the activist and contemplative ways are brought together in the way of life. A new, holistic, integral contract is drawn up, and the two ways stop being separate things, either in tension (as in duality) or in balance (as in mutuality); they are now two dimensions of one thing (in a kind of theological integrity or integrality). Heaven (the afterlife) and earth (this life) stop being perceived as two separate things; they are two dimensions of the experience of God, two venues of the presence of God, two facets of one gift.

Of course, no diagram can adequately convey this. But for now these diagrams can help your intuition begin to see the various ways of spiritual formation come together in an integral way. If you do, you have begun finding your way again, and you are helping us all shift from deep trouble to deep life.

SPIRITUAL EXERCISES

1. Reflect on your beliefs about heaven and hell. Do you believe God's primary concern is this life or the afterlife? Do you agree with the author's perspective or resist it? Why? If you think he is oversimplifying, why might he be doing so intentionally?
2. Go back to the three metaphors of firefighter, health care worker, and social worker. Flesh out these metaphors in relation to the spiritual life.
3. Review the three diagrams and try to explain what they represent in your own words. How do you see these diagrams and the processes they represent to be relevant to your life, your faith community, and the church at large in your lifetime?
4. Write or say aloud a prayer that reflects the mutuality described in this chapter.

PART 2
PRACTICES

CHAPTER 9

PRACTICE MAKES POSSIBLE

One of the truly happy days of my life occurred in October 2004. That was the day my oldest child, Rachel, ran a marathon. I was about to break open with pride—and not just for her, but also for her boyfriend (now husband, Jesse), and as well for her circle of friends who had trained and now were running together. I should mention that about thirty thousand people ran in that Marine Corps Marathon that day along with Rachel, Jesse, and friends, and to tell you the truth, I was proud of all thirty thousand of them, including the few who didn't make it to the finish line. At least they tried!

We met up with Rachel at several agreed-upon points, estimating when she would reach each milestone based on when she crossed the starting line and her normal running speed. We'd try to arrive a little early and then scan the crowds of runners for a few minutes; then we'd start screaming and cheering with absolute abandon when her face came into view.

My wife, Grace, and I met Rachel at the finish line. She looked glorious—and exhausted. While she caught her breath and had something to drink, we waited for the rest of her running mates to make it to the finish line. She was sweaty, but I gave her about ten huge, proud hugs anyway, effusing again and again how proud I was of my little girl (now twenty-three), how much joy she had brought me by training and running and finishing. She replied, still a little breathless, "You know, Dad, you could do this too."

Of course, I couldn't have. If I tried to run a marathon, at about mile three, I would collapse onto the road, a whimpering, groaning, pathetic, panting, gasping, semiconscious subhuman cramp. I told her this, but she replied, "But if you train . . . if you train for six months, you could do it. I did. You'd just have to decide and then train."

MOST OF THE TRULY IMPORTANT SKILLS WE LEARN IN LIFE COME THROUGH TRAINING, PRACTICE, AND TRADITION OR COMMUNITY.

One of my mentors contrasts deciding and trying with training. Deciding is necessary, he says. Nobody finds out they've accidentally trained for a marathon for six months without intending to. But deciding isn't enough, as all of us who have decided to lose weight know. I could even add to my deciding a healthy dose of trying: Sincerely! Passionately! With great commitment and resolution! But unless I put between my decision and the starting line sufficient training of the right sort, it will be "Marathon—26.5, Brian—0" on race day.

That same mentor defines *training* like this: employing appropriate actions within our power by which we become capable of doing things currently beyond our power, and by which we become people we are currently incapable of being. Those "appropriate actions" we could further define as *practices*. And the community of people who teach us the practices we could define as a *community of practice* that carries on the *tradition*. Since we'll be using these terms for the rest of the book, it might be a good idea to review this paragraph once or twice before moving on.

Most of the truly important skills we learn in life come through training, practice, and tradition or community. For example, we didn't learn to speak our native tongue by deciding or trying, but by training. We didn't even realize that we were in training, and our parents (who were our community of practice, carrying on the tradition of English or Chinese or Zulu or whatever) probably didn't even realize that they were training us most of the time. But each time they spoke to us, saying "bottle" and then holding up "bottle," they were training us, engaging in the age-old practice of holding up a thing and saying the word for it. We were learning the English, Chinese, or Zulu way of communication. Similarly, when they withheld something from us until we said "please" and "thank you," they were the community training us in the tradition of community, and we were practicing so that the way of courtesy would become natural to us.

It took a couple of years of practice, but in the process, largely without realizing it, we became fluent speakers of our native tongue, and maybe we became courteous people, to boot. Without the community, without the tradition, and without the practice, neither possibility would have been actualized.

Later, we may have decided to learn to play the violin or soccer, or to master calculus or trout fishing or tai chi. In each case, our decision required us to find the community that carried the tradition and then to enter into the practice of that community and tradition by submitting ourselves to the authority of masters in the tradition, namely, the teachers in the community of violin, soccer, calculus, trout fishing, or tai chi.

Interestingly, the practices of the desired art or way are generally not the same as the way itself, especially in the beginning. For example, one doesn't learn to play Mozart on the violin by playing Mozart on the violin. One learns Mozart by starting with this tacky blue book that was written, not by Mozart, but by some unknown and not-all-that-skilled music teacher from North Dakota or Missouri or somewhere far from Vienna named Jane Mildow. Inside *Jane Mildow's Violin Book for Absolute Beginners, Level 1A*, one doesn't find lines from Mozart, but exercises to develop note-reading skills and bowing skills and fingering skills and so on. By the time one can play reasonably well, she may have all but forgotten who Mozart is, because she's been so focused on Jane Mildow's levels 1A through 1F, then levels 2A through 2E, and so on. Rediscovering Mozart may come as something of a surprise.

I experienced this twice in my musical career. I remember exactly when and where I decided to learn the clarinet. It was while listening to an old LP (an archaic form of music recording, for those raised on iPods and MP3s) of Prokofiev's *Peter and the Wolf.* I never even knew that Prokofiev was the composer until a few minutes ago when I looked it up, but here's what I knew: the clarinet part touched my seven-year-old heart, and someday, I wanted to play that part. I translated, "I want the beautiful sound of the clarinet in *Peter and the Wolf* to become part of my life" to "I want to take clarinet lessons." Something similar happened when I heard a student from my primary school play Ellmenreich's "Spinning Song." I wanted that song to be part of my life, so I chose to restart the piano lessons I had complained about and hated.

In neither case did I want to practice. And it wasn't just that I wanted to play either. What I really wanted was for these songs to *be* me, and I wanted to *be* them and to become the kind of person in whom these songs were alive, ready to be played by heart at any moment. This vision—of myself as containing these songs and being inhabited by them, of myself with these songs playing through my own fingers, and on the strings and reeds of my heart—prompted me to submit to the traditions of clarinet and piano, taking on the practices with all of their frustration and challenge and, sometimes, tedium.

I think this is what happens to all of us when we feel a pull toward God. Not many of us, I think, feel really excited about attending church or singing religious songs or stopping the snarky comments or disciplining ourselves to pray. What we feel is that some music is missing from our lives, and we need it; we can't be fully ourselves as we hope to be without it. There's a "rumor of glory" out there (to borrow Bruce Cockburn's beautiful phrase), and we can't live without the glory. So we make the decision and take on the practices because of the dream or vision of a life that is impossible for us as we are, a life we can't live without. We set out to become someone we can't currently be simply by deciding or trying, and we do so by taking on practices in a community that carries the tradition that has won our heart.

WHAT WE FEEL IS THAT SOME MUSIC IS MISSING FROM OUR LIVES, AND WE NEED IT; WE CAN'T BE FULLY OURSELVES AS WE HOPE TO BE WITHOUT IT.

At some point, we become so enthralled with the tradition that we are eager to learn its practices for their own sake, but I think this desire expresses our confidence that the tradition has reasons for its practices, and we trust the tradition enough to engage in practices that we can't pretend to understand.

In my own experience, fasting exemplifies this trust in the tradition. Anyone who has seen my waistline knows that I won't be accused of asceticism in regard to food. But years ago I began the practice of fasting . . . for a meal, for three meals, even for a few days on a few occasions. I don't do this religiously, but rather occasionally. Anyway, when I fast, I don't in any way feel closer to God.

In fact, when I fast, I mostly feel closer to pizza. And glazed doughnuts. And tortilla chips. When I simply miss a couple of meals, they call to me, they haunt me, they stimulate culinary fantasies that in turn stimulate my salivary glands, and if that sounds a little sicko, I suppose it is. And maybe that's the point of fasting, I'm realizing.

For example, a couple of years ago I had decided to fast on a certain day. I was running errands, and I found myself driving into a Dunkin' Donuts store and buying a glazed doughnut, something I seldom do when I'm not fasting. I had taken one bite out of the sugar-fat confection when I remembered, *Shoot! I was supposed to be fasting today!* The proverbial red devil with his pitchfork and arrow tail was predictably perched in whispering distance to my ear, and you can guess what he said: *Well, you've already blown it! Might as well eat the whole thing. While you're at it, those bear claws look pretty good, and you haven't had a jelly-filled sugar doughnut in years, and I think your blood levels for chocolate are kind of low, so you probably need a chocolate crème-filled too.*

Meanwhile, in the other ear came the sound of my better angel's howling laughter. Instead of feeling mad at myself or guilty, I was totally amused.

Even though I didn't have the foggiest notion of exactly how fasting was supposed to work, somehow that moment of laughing at myself told me that even though I was failing at fasting, the practice of fasting was succeeding. I smiled, threw the doughnut away, and got back on the wagon with my fast for the rest of the day.

Nobody ever explained to me how fasting is supposed to work; the "rules of the art" of fasting weren't known explicitly to me or to the mentors (*masters* in Polanyi's lexicon)[1] who told me I should do it. I just trusted my mentors and the tradition they represented, even though I couldn't "analyze and account in detail for its effectiveness." Now, based on my experience, if you asked me how the practice of fasting works, here's what I'd say . . . admitting quickly that my understanding of fasting is probably more developed than my actual resistance to doughnuts, and that's kind of sad.

During that day of fasting, *I felt and acknowledged my weakness in the face of impulses and cravings from my body.* Doing so was so humbling that it erupted in a good laugh at myself. The laughter expressed a kind of sympathy for myself, I think, like when we laugh at someone who trips and falls or otherwise embarrasses himself. And it also expressed, I think, a kind of joy in learning something, an acknowledgment that I had little idea how much my life was controlled by bodily appetites. At least at that moment, through the subconscious magnetism of sugar and fat that drew me into the parking lot, into the store, and up to the counter, I had a better idea of my weakness than I did before. The giant Goliath in the biblical story was felled by a single smooth stone, and my willpower was felled by the pleasure contained in a single bite of a glazed doughnut. At that moment it became a little harder to be proud of my exploits as a pastor or author.

Second, when I fasted that day, *I practiced impulse control.* Of course, I didn't even know how out-of-control my impulses were until I had taken the first hundred-calorie bite. But when I dropped those five hundred remaining calories of delight into the trash can, I said a completely unheroic, embarrassed, and humbled no to my craving.

Simultaneously, *I asserted to myself the importance of something other than impulse gratification.* In this case, the "something other than impulse gratification" was a kind of vague desire for spiritual growth . . . maybe not very impressive, but at least better than a doughnut.

Fasting that day also helped me *trade something I could see for something I couldn't.* Somehow, admitting (with a laugh) my spiritual poverty and weakness of will opened me up to receive a different kind of sweetness and satisfaction. Again, I didn't know exactly what that sweetness and satisfaction might be, but because of my trust in my community of mentors and the tradition they carried, I had a hunch it would be worthwhile.

PRACTICE MAKES POSSIBLE SOME THINGS THAT WOULD OTHERWISE HAVE BEEN IMPOSSIBLE.

Now, I look back on my occasional small experiments in fasting over the years and feel my hunch was validated. I think back to last week, when someone sent me a link to a website where a critic of my work indulged in some high-flying religious character assassination. My reaction to being misrepresented, insulted, and mocked (this website did all three) was quite literally visceral. I felt something tighten in my gut, strangely similar in some ways to the craving for a chocolate-covered glazed doughnut. I started thinking about ways I could get back at this fellow, things I could write that would prove to him and to all virtual reality who the better man is. It was a kind of hunger . . . for revenge, I'm ashamed to say, and for self-justification, and to win and to hurt rather than lose and be hurt.

And sitting here now, I wonder if my ability to let that feeling go last week didn't have something to do with letting five hundred calories of delight drop behind the Thank You sign on a trash can door one day. A little practice at impulse control, a little practice at facing my weakness, a little practice at laughing at my pretensions to maturity and spirituality, and a new possibility was actualized . . . thanks to a tradition carried by a community, embodied in some mentors who shared "elbow knowledge" with me, a slightly chubby guy with a sweet tooth, who is still overly concerned about his reputation but yet wants to follow Jesus and become more of what he was and is.

They say that practice makes perfect, but I wouldn't know about that. What I do know is that practice makes possible some things that would otherwise have been impossible.

SPIRITUAL EXERCISES

1. Take the main metaphors of this chapter—training to run a marathon, training to speak a language, training to play an instrument—and look for similarities with the spiritual life.
2. If you've never tried fasting, try it for one day this week. Don't read a book about it (yet—you'll want to do that later). Don't tell anyone about it. Just do it. And see what you learn through the experience.
3. The author describes an experience in which he laughed at himself or perhaps laughed with himself. How could this kind of laughter be therapeutic? What would some less helpful alternatives have been? Look for a chance to laugh good-naturedly at yourself sometime soon.
4. The author describes his desire to learn to play two songs—or

to have two songs become part of his life—or to become the kind of person who has these two songs in his life. Can you recall a similar experience in your life? What can that experience tell you about your spiritual life?

5. Write or speak aloud a prayer that tells God what kind of person you want to become, and what kind of music you want to fill your life and flow out of you.

CHAPTER 10

CONTEMPLATIVE PRACTICES

During my life, I think I've lost about 200 pounds. The most I've ever weighed was about 210, so as a math whiz (or not), you've already realized that I've regained most of what I've lost, several times over, or perhaps you could say that I've lost most of my losses to subsequent gains. Anyway, based on what I've said about my experience with fasting, you have some idea why and how this has happened, even though I have hardly mentioned my paramount dietary nemesis: tortilla chips.

My wife and I are currently losing some weight together. I secretly suspect that she's only pretending to lose weight in order to get me to do so, which is yet another sign of her love, because she has never looked overweight to me. (I really mean this and am not just saying it in hopes that she'll read it.) Be that as it may, she has entered (on our joint behalf) a community that upholds a particular tradition of weight loss and that embodies and teaches a set of time-tested, helpful, and doable practices about which this community is quick to say, "We're not talking about a diet. This is a new way of life." I think this is probably true, especially in the sense that embracing a new way of life will produce sustainable gains (er, I mean losses), while embarking on a series of short-term diets will result in losing 200 pounds over thirty years but gaining back 170 or 240 pounds or whatever.

This community's practices include a weekly gathering to share stories and experiences, exchange inspiration and practical tips, and weigh in—which for most people most weeks is a cause for celebration because success is defined as losing as little as 0.1 pound, so it's about progress, not perfection. They also teach the practice of reading labels for fat content, fiber content, calorie totals, and so on. They offer a handy chart that integrates calories, fiber, and fat to give you a point value for each kind of food you're considering consuming. (Neither tortilla chips nor doughnuts have impressive numbers on this chart, as you no doubt guessed.)

Recalling our earlier consideration of open-source spirituality, this weight loss tradition, like the twelve-step recovery movement, has a core practice of turning experienced practitioners into mentors. It doesn't create a special class of "weight loss clergy," but encourages each practitioner to encourage others in a kind of Reformation-esque "priesthood of all the practitioners." One other fascinating practice of this community and tradition: they institutionalize "cheating" by giving you a bunch of extra "points" to perhaps sneak in a few tortilla chips per week—kind of a weekly Mardi Gras. You have a mixture of law and grace.

If you ask the mentors in this community how much grace you can enjoy—how strict and careful you have to be about your eating habits, weight, and general health—they'll say the answer depends on a lot of things: your genetics, your cultural environment, your gender and age, your lifetime eating habits and their cumulative effects on you, your current eating habits, your pattern of exercise, your support system, your work habits, your sleeping habits and stress level, your particular eating nemeses, and so on. Based on their bank of experience as a weight loss community, they can offer you general parameters for your corporeal transformation, and beyond that, they have mentors to help you develop, sustain, and adapt as necessary the unique mix of practices to reach your individual goals—spiritual direction, if you will.

If some of us come out of denial about our need to lose some character flab and tone up our virtues (have you ever noticed the etymological connection between *virtue* and *virility*?), if we realize that as we've been getting older we've been getting bitter instead of better, we will reach a point of deciding to improve the health of our souls. Perhaps after some procrastination and failed attempts to go it alone, we'll realize that we need to enter a community that upholds a particular tradition of spiritual life and that embodies and teaches a set of time-tested, helpful, and doable practices. This community may well say, "We're not just talking about a religion. This is a new way of life," and they'll be telling the truth.

The Christian tradition offers a wide array of practices to those seeking to improve or sustain the health and well-being of their souls. As we saw earlier, many of these practices have been clustered under the category called *contemplative*.

The Christian contemplative tradition draws from the wisdom tradition of the Hebrew Scriptures; it seeks to avoid the shallowness, ignorance, and destructiveness of the people called *fools* in the book of Proverbs, for example. It also draws from the Greek philosophical tradition, where philosophy is literally the *love of wisdom*—with clear resonances with the Hebrew wisdom tradition. Near the head of this tradition stands Socrates, for whom the unexamined life is not worth living. Two generations later, Aristotle expands on Socrates' *examined life* and speaks of the *contemplative life*. The good life of happiness, well-being, or living well, he says, is possible for those who give themselves to the practices of contemplation.

Although it draws from both these ancient resources, the taproot of the Christian contemplative tradition goes deep into the writings of the New Testament. The New Testament documents emphasize the reality of incarnation—that God desires to enter the human being, body and soul, so that, like Jesus, we become bearers of the Holy Spirit, reaching toward the unimaginable "spiritual event horizon" of being *filled to all the fullness of God* (Ephesians 3:19; Colossians 2:10). This language of fullness resonates deeply with rich imagery of unification and interpenetration so common in the New Testament. Although this language has sometimes been reduced to forensic categories in some Christian traditions, the contemplative and mystical traditions explore its full inscape, pushing to the frontier of the spiritually erotic and beyond—a daring characteristic that, by the way, the Christian contemplative tradition shares with the Sufi tradition in Islam:

- We are "one" with and in Christ. (Ephesians 4:4–6, 15–16)
- Christ is in us, and we are in Christ. (Colossians 1:27–28)
- We are the bride of Christ. (Ephesians 5:32)
- We receive the "seed" of Christ. (1 John 3:9)

In essence, the contemplative tradition—in its Eastern Orthodox, Roman Catholic, Protestant, and Pentecostal forms—claims with all Christian traditions that human beings can be forgiven by and reconciled to God, preparing the way for a glorious afterlife. But it goes farther: the contemplative tradition claims that we human beings can also *experience* the living God in this life in ways that range from gentle and subtle to dramatic, ravishing, and electrifying.

In classic contemplative literature, these experiences of God are often described as "favors" or "visitations" of God. They are consistently received as gifts from God, never tricks conjurable by magic incantations or esoteric arts. They are mysteries that can never be reduced to equations or formulas or techniques.

And this distinction—between gifts, mysteries, favors, or visitations on the one side and tricks, magic, equations, formulas, and techniques on the other—makes all the difference in the ancient way of spiritual practice. The latter cluster of words suggests a way that humans can overpower God; the former, a way that God's goodness can overpower the ignorance, resistance, obliviousness, and meanness of human beings. The latter words evoke an economic setting, where we earn payments from God, manipulating God into a position where God must comply to our wishes. In contrast, the former words suggest an intimate and relational setting, where our efforts—meaning spiritual practices that we engage in— are real, but never understood as a form of earning or buying.[1] A man may bring flowers and chocolates and songs to express his love for his beloved, and we smile. But if he brings cash to buy sex from her, we shake our heads. The distinction may be hard to quantify, but it means the difference between romance and prostitution.

Imagine a great violinist who gives two hundred concerts a year. Let's say that three of her concerts were disastrous—she had the flu, or her bridge broke in the middle of the evening, or a fire alarm buzzed five minutes into her first song. Let's say that 190 of her concerts were good—some stronger than others, but the crowds were satisfied. And what were the remaining seven concerts? They were exceptional, the reviewers might say: inspired, transcendent, ecstatic. They might even use the term *magical*, but of course they don't mean it in a literal sense. They mean that some inexplicable things converged that night, and the music somehow unleashed latent power that was unknown the other 193 nights.

The violinist herself can't explain this. She feels on those nights that she has been taken up to a higher level, that on those seven nights, a glorious mystery has filled her and the audience and the sound waves that connect them. She may not even want to speak of it, because doing so somehow cheapens the experience. She knows that what happened those nights was not simply in her power; she was every bit as prepared, practiced, serious, committed, and dedicated the other nights as well.

CONTEMPLATIVE PRACTICES . . .

ARE MEANS BY WHICH WE

BECOME PREPARED FOR

GRACE TO SURPRISE US.

Now, if we take her seriously when she says those seven nights were a gift, we could try an experiment. We could substitute for our master violinist an amateur, or even a pretty good violinist, and those nights simply wouldn't happen. This paradox—that skill and practice and experience are necessary conditions, but not sufficient conditions—is a paradox known well to people in the contemplative spiritual tradition, just as it is to musicians, artists, teachers, preachers, comedians, dancers, and anyone involved in work that can be labeled "inspired" or "uninspired."

You could put it like this: the gift never stops being a gift, but the gift "happens" to those who are practiced in ways it doesn't typically happen to those who aren't. As soon as the practitioner presumes that the gift is actually earnable or achievable through a formula or equation, the performances lose their magic and descend from art to propaganda, from being authentically moving to being predictably manipulative. It's like the person who says, "I've noticed that good coincidences happen more when I'm prepared than when I'm not."

Contemplative practices, then, are means by which we become prepared for grace to surprise us. They are ways of opening our hands so that we can receive the gifts God wants to give us. There is no single authoritative list of contemplative practices, but lists generally include the following practices, which are exercised more or less in solitude, making the first cluster in many ways the key to the rest:

- Solitude, Sabbath, and Silence: Resting in the presence of God, without work or speech, so one becomes more aware of the companionship, grace, and love of God than one has been of the companionship, demands, and duties associated with other people.
- Spiritual Reading and Study: Exercising the mind to love God through the reading and study of Scripture and other spiritual literature.
- Spiritual Direction or Spiritual Friendship: In privacy and confidentiality, opening one's inner life to a mentor or peer to gain guidance, accountability, and encouragement in the spiritual journey.
- Practicing God's Presence: Learning to be aware of God as constant companion, staying in constant contact with God, living with one's spiritual windows and doors open to God.
- Fixed-Hour Prayer: "Stealing away," as the old songs say, at certain points in the day to be in contact with God through common prayers.
- Prayer Journaling: Writing prayers and keeping them for future review.
- Contemplative Prayer: Practicing a kind of prayer that culminates in silent attentiveness to God, a prayer that is about listening and receiving rather than speaking and expressing.
- Service, Secrecy, and Generosity: Serving and giving to others

anonymously so that, in the spirit of "your left hand not knowing what your right hand is doing" (Matthew 6:3), those being served don't know who served them, and they receive a true gift—one that carries with it no strings of obligation to say thanks or repay the favor. These gifts are given for the benefit of the person in need, but also to God, who counts kindness to the poor and needy as kindness done to God.

- Simplicity and Slowness: Resisting the pull of complexity, acquisition, consumption, and hurry through deliberately choosing a simple and slow life—in dress, eating, transportation, technology, speech, and so on.
- Fasting and Self-Denial: Reducing the consumption of food or other pleasures as a way of strengthening spiritual health and resolve—often on certain days imbued by the faith community with certain meanings.
- Feasting and Celebration: Increasing the consumption of food or other pleasures as a way of strengthening spiritual health and joy—often on certain days imbued by the faith community with certain meanings.
- Holy Days and Seasons: Observing special days and seasons that interrupt the normalcy and regularity of daily life with intensity. These special days or seasons stimulate the remembering of special events or meanings and provide members of a faith community with a special encouragement to engage in specified spiritual practices.
- Submission: Decisively accepting the limitations set by a fallible human being or an unpleasant situation as a way of weakening self-will and pride.
- Gratitude: Counting one's blessings and resisting the tendency to turn blessings into entitlements or take blessings for granted, through table grace and other forms of prayer.

• Meditation and Memorization: Holding a truth in the mind through nonanxious concentration so that it can be savored and rooted deeply and accessible to memory in the stress and struggle of daily life.

Again, lists like these should be seen as options available to us, not as requirements imposed on us. They could be compared to the exercise equipment we find at a health club. They're not the only ways to get exercise, but they're inventions of the community of faith that has been at this for a long time, tools available to us to help us develop our potential. They can help us strengthen certain muscle groups in our souls. They can help us burn excess calories to save us from becoming spiritually flabby. By using them, we prepare ourselves to receive "the good coincidences" of life: the priceless, quiet gift of well-being; the gentle habit of living deep and loving well; and sometimes, even, the lightning strike of inspiration or ecstasy that arcs by surprise into our souls from the fullness of God.

SPIRITUAL EXERCISES

1. Reflect on the spiritual life as participation in a weight loss program (or, if you prefer, an addiction recovery program). What are your "dietary nemeses"? What are the doughnuts and tortilla chips that tempt you to "fall off the wagon"?
2. Look over the list of contemplative practices. Compare them to exercise equipment in a health club. What muscles would each practice help exercise and strengthen? Which practices have you had the most experience with? The least? Which would you like to experiment with?
3. Review the ways in which the Christian contemplative tradition

draws from Hebrew wisdom literature, Greek philosophical literature, and the uniquely Christian understanding of the incarnation. How could these three be in tension? How can they be in harmony?

4. Contrast the ideas of effort and earning.

5. Reflect on the imagery of unity and intimacy that pushes beyond "frontier of the spiritually erotic." Let this holy imagery of intercourse and mutual indwelling inspire a prayer, perhaps in the form of a love poem or a love letter from your deepest being to God.

CHAPTER 11

COMMUNAL PRACTICES

Distinctions are hard to make; lines are hard to draw. As soon as you define or delineate something, you find flapping shirttails and loose ends crossing over and not staying tucked in and tied up, and that's how I feel as I try to describe the practices of the spiritual life. We've spoken of the practices of the *via contemplativa*, or the contemplative way, in the last chapter, and in the next chapter we'll speak of the practices of the *via activa*, or the activist way. But in between there is this other category: the communal way. If the via contemplativa is about the upward journey—where we descend into our deepest soul and then from there rise upward toward God, and if the via activa is about the outward journey—where we express our inner transformation in the outward world, then the way of community is about

> **THE WAY OF COMMUNITY IS ABOUT THE INWARD JOURNEY, NOT THE JOURNEY INTO *ME* BUT THE JOURNEY INTO *WE*.**

the inward journey, not the journey into *me* but the journey into *we*. Or perhaps we should more accurately say that all three journeys are adventures into God, but that the upward, inward, and outward journeys explore God in solitude, in community, and in service, respectively.

In the previous chapter, we saw some practices leaning into this category—spiritual direction, for example, is a step from solitary practice into communal practice, and feasting is communal in a way that fasting is not. Study can be both solitary and communal, and in fact each is enriched by the other. Even the act of reading, though done alone, brings together writer and reader in a kind of virtual community, and in some way people who have read the same books are brought together into another kind of community. Further, nobody could learn the contemplative or solitary practices if those practices weren't preserved in a community and passed on across time and space.

So, although their centers of gravity are different, there is plenty of overlap in the contemplative way and the communal way. The communal way is centered in faith communities—formal churches, synagogues, and mosques, and also less formal or institutional but no less important communities, such as small groups, circles of friends, reading groups, online groups, and so on. If you think about the contemplative way as a solo art or sport—playing the piano, painting, rock climbing, fishing, bowling—you could think of the communal way as a team art or sport—playing in a symphony, dancing in a troupe, acting in a play, basketball, football (either kind), volleyball.

So, it's impossible and pointless to draw clear lines to separate contemplative and communal practices into sealed categories. Golfers, for example, can play on a foursome against another foursome. But there's a difference between adding individual scores in golf and only being able to score through teamwork in basketball. Similarly, a percussionist will practice in private for her role in the symphony, but private practice can't substitute for practicing with the whole orchestra any more than a dancer's private rehearsal can substitute for practice with the troupe.

If the quiet place of prayer—a closet or study, a bench in a garden, a narrow path through a forest, a cup of coffee and an open journal and Bible at the kitchen table—could represent the contemplative practices, the meeting of the gathered community can symbolize the communal practices, whether we imagine a monastery, a country chapel, a great cathedral, or an informal faith community meeting in a home or pub. As people gather for what is popularly called the "worship service" or "going to church," they are engaging—usually without realizing it—in the *via communitiva*. If spiritual practices are actions within our power that help us become the kinds of people who can do things currently beyond our power, then "going to church" means gathering for communal spiritual practices, engaging in a kind of group workout, if you will. In so doing, the community that carries on a way of life and its practices calls people together weekly or seasonally or annually to reaffirm their commitment and practice being a community.

In fact, the word *liturgy* suggests as much. The word literally means "the work of the people." This is commonly understood to mean that people do the work of praying, singing, listening, speaking, kneeling, and so on. Let me offer a slight modification. What if we define *liturgy* to mean "the workout of the people"?

In this way, our traditions and gifted liturgists offer us time-tested and skillfully designed workouts, just as an aerobics or tai chi instructor or vocal coach might. The goal is to help us maintain our spiritual health and strength, and more, to stretch us and challenge us

LITURGY IS A THOUGHTFULLY DESIGNED, TIME-TESTED SET AND ORDER OF COMMUNAL SPIRITUAL PRACTICES THAT MUST BE ADAPTED AND UPDATED AS NEEDED FOR THE TIMES AND COMMUNITIES IN WHICH IT IS EMPLOYED

to new levels of health and strength, grace and balance, endurance and performance. In this way, then, our liturgy—and remember, churches that don't have a written liturgy still have a liturgy, but it's just unwritten—isn't simply something written in stone, determined by tradition or religious powers-that-be. Rather, liturgy is a thoughtfully designed, time-tested set and order of communal spiritual practices that must be adapted and updated as needed for the times and communities in which it is employed.

Yes, I know that too few people understand "going to church" in this way—too few attendees, and worse, too few pastors, worship leaders, and liturgists. But it wouldn't take long for us to change people's thinking in this regard. Let me offer a few examples and suggestions, describing a typical church service in terms of a thoughtful ordering of practices.

ARRIVAL PRACTICES

Inconvenience. Showing up is inherently inconvenient. It means going to a place I didn't choose at a time I didn't choose for a purpose I do choose. My commitment to the purpose—in this case, learning and living a way of life—motivates me to show up. In this way, going to church when you don't feel like it becomes the most important kind of going to church there is.

Self-preparation. Our daily self-preparation typically involves showering, brushing teeth, grooming hair (if one is so fortunate as to have hair to groom), choosing clothing, and so on. Preparation for the gathering of the faith community would, one could predict, involve additional kinds of self-preparation, which might take the form of prayer, reading, or even discussion in the car about why joining and showing up in a faith community is important.

Hospitality. As one arrives at a gathering—in the parking lot, on the sidewalk—others are arriving too, and how one treats them is, it turns out, a highly significant communal practice. If one habitually treats them as strangers—say, as one might treat strangers pushing carts down an aisle in a grocery store, or strangers sitting in the waiting room at the dentist, or strangers boarding a Boeing 747—then one is practicing a way of treating people that may or may not be in line with the way of this community. Interestingly, it was precisely this so-called detail—of how we welcome one another when we gather—that was of great concern to the first apostles (1 Corinthians 11; James 2). For example, Paul's call to "greet one another with a holy kiss" (repeated four times in his epistles) was more significant than it appears. Class-conscious Roman society required that people only exchange the kiss with peers, but the early churches brought together Jew and Gentile, men and women, slave and free, rich and poor. That people transgressed (or transcended) normal social convention was essential to the early church in maintaining its higher allegiance to the way of Jesus instead of the way of Rome.

ENGAGEMENT PRACTICES

Stillness. As one enters the gathering space—whether it's a stained-glass cathedral, a humble chapel, a rented elementary school cafeteria, a living room, or a booth at a pub—one can practice stillness, quieting one's internal chatter so that one can truly listen, letting the dust of hurry and worry settle so that one can simply be present and awake. Churches often use prelude music to assist in this practice of stilling and quieting the soul, reminiscent of the beautiful poem found in Psalm 131. No doubt, some kinds of music can be counterproductive, but my sense is that wherever it occurs in the gathering, without the practice of stillness we aren't getting the workout we need. Not coming together at all is a practice. Coming together and talking, talking, talking, with no stillness at all, is a practice. Coming together and enjoying stillness as well as speech is yet another practice, and in it, precious things can happen.

Invocation. Oddly, many of our invocations ask ridiculous things. They ask God to be present—as if God wasn't present already. They tell God we're coming into God's presence, as if we weren't in God's presence before we gathered, or as if he didn't notice until we told him. But beneath these rather clumsy expressions is an important reality: we are often oblivious to God's presence, asleep at the wheel as it were. The invocation is a way for us as a community to say that we are together seeking to wake up intentionally to the reality that has always been true: that God is with us and we are with God, living and moving and having our being in God. And when the invocation is either recited in unison or in a responsive way, we also affirm that we are waking up intentionally *together.*

The way we participate in an invocation may be as important as whether or not we practice it. For example, probably the oldest

Christian liturgical element we have is an invocation that goes something like this:

> **Leader:** The Lord be with you.
> **Group:** And also with you.
> **Leader:** Lift up your hearts.
> **Group:** We lift up our hearts to the Lord.
> **Leader:** It is good and right to give God thanks and praise.

Imagine leader and people mouthing these words in the echoing, deadening monotone of heartless, formulaic, institutional dreariness. Then imagine leader and people exclaiming the same words with enthusiasm, maybe even at the volume of a shout or cheer. Then imagine the same words being said with the hushed intensity of people telling one another an amazing secret. Same words—three very different practices.

Singing. Singing is so familiar in our churches that I fear we are missing what a miracle it is. First, singing involves our bodies—and to be uncomfortably specific—it involves mucous and spit, vibrating vocal cords, lips, teeth, tongues, lungs, and diaphragms. Second, it involves our souls—our hearts, minds, volition—"all that is within me," in the words of the psalmist (103:1 NRSV). Third, it involves a text, sometimes (though too rarely) a beautiful poetic lyric. Fourth, it involves a score, sometimes (again, too rarely) a beautiful artistic score. Fifth, that score engages instruments—whether organ or drum, guitar or piano, trumpet or didgeridoo. Sixth, it often involves parts—call-and-response parts, or soprano-alto-tenor-bass harmonies. And finally, it involves other people—many voices, one song. Think of it: bodies and souls, people and instruments, texts and notes, men and women and children, Republicans and Democrats, liberals and conservatives somehow coming together in the miracle of a song or hymn. Figuratively as literally, songs harmonize us, which is why they are such important communal spiritual practices.

As well, songs (like acts of romantic affection) simultaneously express and intensify emotion. Sadly, the singing in some of our churches expresses a range of emotion that runs from B to C (bored to complacent), but the Bible takes us from A (angry) to F (fervent) to J (joyful) to L (lamenting) to N (nostalgic) to R (restful) to X (er, exalted) to Z (zealous). I'm glad to report that people are beginning to notice the narrow range of songs used in so many of our churches, whether they be "traditional" or "contemporary" or "blended," and even better, they're starting to write new songs that more fully explore and express the spiritual life in both content and emotion.

LISTENING PRACTICES

Attentiveness. I've preached enough sermons to add a new verse to the old Joni Mitchell song: Points and stories, shouts and tears/ inspiring hope and calming fears/ a moment's insight lasts for years, I've seen sermons that way/ But sometimes they're a tiresome chore/ predictable clichés that bore/ Why do they keep coming back for more, Sunday after Sunday/ I've looked at sermons from both sides now.[1]

I've come to see the preparing and listening to sermons as a communal practice of attentiveness, where the speaker, preacher, or whomever begins by simultaneously attending to the Scriptures, the faith community, his or her own soul, and the larger world in which they are all situated, listening for resonances that indicate places where God may be speaking. The people similarly come, attending to resonances between the text, the sermon, and their own lives, seeking in that resonance to integrate sacred theology and personal biography and shared history. The whole process—preparation, delivery, reception, memory—is a shared spiritual practice by which the whole congregation (again, this seems like a miracle that we often take for granted) engages in a shared practice of listening to God.

Such a practice betrays a deep and understated creed: *We believe that God is real. We believe that God understands us and wishes to be understood by us. We believe that God mysteriously but truly speaks to us to promote mutual understanding. We believe that there are ways we can hear God interdependently, together, that we cannot hear God independently, alone* (which does not preclude the opposite also being true).

I'VE COME TO SEE THE PREPARING AND LISTENING TO SERMONS AS A COMMUNAL PRACTICE OF ATTENTIVENESS.

When I'm sermonizing on this subject, I often ask people what question would come to mind if God sent them the following message: *I will give you a message of great importance sometime during a sermon in the next three years.* They always reply with this question: "Which Sunday?" After all, they don't want to miss the big week. About this time, they always laugh, because they anticipate the follow-up question I've got coming down the chute: what if the only way you'll be prepared to hear that message when it comes is by practicing attentiveness for the next 155 Sundays?

Interpretation and Discernment. When people listen to sermons, prayers, songs, even announcements, they're not simply passive receivers. They're constantly, though often barely consciously, carrying on a dialogue with the message and messenger. Amens and hallelujahs are the tip of the iceberg of response, but underneath the surface, what's often unspoken would be articulated more as, *Yeah, right!* Or, *So what?* Or, *That's what you say.* Or, *No way!* Or, *Burn, heretic, burn!* Or, *Who cares?* Or, *What planet is he from?* Or, *How long until kickoff?*

Students of hermeneutics often speak of a hermeneutic of suspicion. With a hermeneutic—or interpretive approach—of suspicion, we listen to a sermon or other utterance, looking for ways to unmask its hidden errors, biases, inconsistencies, and so on. We receive the messenger and message the way we might receive a sales pitch from a networking marketer. The hermeneutic of suspicion intends to correct its opposite, a naive or precritical hermeneutic by which one receives a message as authoritative.[2]

Confession and Assurance of Pardon. I include confession as a listening practice because it involves a dimension of what Parker Palmer calls listening to your life, in this case, listening to your conscience. Having heard the word, we admit that we are indeed part of the problem, and doing so is—once again—more miraculous than we commonly realize. It's quite an amazing thing for a group of people who have dedicated themselves to becoming better, to say, in public, in unison, that they aren't.

The power of communal confession came home to me a few years ago when a man began attending the church where I was pastor. He had held a responsible position in business and had also developed a secret addiction that led to criminal behavior. Law enforcement, it turned out, had been following his case for years. They showed up at his house one day and left with bags and boxes of evidence, which precipitated a complete meltdown of his life. He resigned from his job in disgrace, awaiting trial and imprisonment, and became acutely suicidal, which is what it sometimes takes to bring people to a church, asking for help. I had met with him in private for counseling and prayer, and one Sunday, I happened to be seated near him when we came to this communal practice of confession in our service. The particular confession we used this day went like this:

Gracious God,
    our sins are too heavy to carry,
    too real to hide,
    and too deep to undo.
Forgive what our lips tremble to name, what our hearts can
      no longer
    bear, and what has become for us a consuming fire of
      judgment.
Set us free from a past that we cannot change;
    open to us a future in which we can be changed;
    and grant us grace to grow more and more in your likeness
      and image,
    through Jesus Christ,
    the light of the world. Amen.

Nobody else knew the drama of what it meant for this man to say these words. But I felt a shudder literally move through him, and I could hear the emotion in his voice, and intuitively I knew that he was experiencing a truth that I, too, have experienced. To frankly, directly speak the painful truth about my own darkness in the presence of God and in the presence of my peers is a powerful thing, a transforming thing. Without this kind of confession, speaking too freely and glibly of forgiveness can turn free grace into cheap grace. With it, an assurance of pardon completes a profound cycle of grace that is to the soul, and to the faith community, what the water cycle is to the biosphere. What could be more wonderful than to listen for and receive the assurance of God's mercy, falling on the dried-out soul like life-giving rain?

We could go on to speak of *response practices* such as the Eucharist, common prayers, intercession, and the offering. Then we could consider *reentry practices*, such as the invitation, community news (aka "announcements"—which are, along with the offering, among the most underrated communal practices of all), the benediction, and after-church hospitality. We could also consider the other settings in which we get a kind of workout in communal practices: home or cell or support groups, retreats, conferences and camps, and family meals. But I think we've made the point well enough: between the realm of private contemplative practices and public missional practices is this realm of shared communal practices that is so easily misunderstood.

TO FRANKLY, DIRECTLY SPEAK THE PAINFUL TRUTH ABOUT MY OWN DARKNESS IN THE PRESENCE OF GOD AND IN THE PRESENCE OF MY PEERS IS A POWERFUL THING, A TRANSFORMING THING.

Some, of course, overemphasize the communal practices, as if being a Christian simply meant going to church. Others, sadly, underemphasize them, and they do so in one of two ways.

First, they may go to church without understanding the potential and purposes of the communal practices they encounter there. As a result, they may engage in spiritual malpractice instead of spiritual practice, leading to spiritual malformation rather than spiritual formation. That's why, according to the apostle Paul, gathering in the wrong way can be worse than not gathering at all: "Now in the following instructions I do not commend you, because when you come together it is not for the better but for the worse" (1 Corinthians 11:17 NRSV). The apostle James erupted in a full-fledged rant along similar lines, suggesting that the common practice of "favoritism" (or cliquishness, a failure to properly practice the presence of people) made him wonder whether the so-called Christians to whom he wrote really got the message of Jesus at all (James 2:1–7).[3]

But others make the opposite mistake, referred to by an unnamed New Testament author. Perhaps they become disillusioned with "organized religion" for legitimate reasons, but their reaction—to withdraw from communal practices altogether—becomes a practice (the writer calls it a *habit*) in and of itself, and not a helpful one: "Let us hold fast to the confession of our hope without wavering, for he who as promised is faithful. And let us consider how to provoke one another to love and good deeds, not neglecting to meet together, as is the habit of some, but encouraging one another, and all the more as you see the Day approaching" (Hebrews 10:23–25 NRSV).

Sustained and sustaining hope, mutual encouragement, and stimulation to love and good deeds—these are among the desired outcomes of communal practices. Without them, we would expect people of faith to become increasingly grim and apathetic—which is just what we all too often see, isn't it?

SPIRITUAL EXERCISES

1. Review the upward, outward, and inward journeys. Of the three, in which do you feel most and least comfortable and experienced?

2. Tell or write your autobiography in relation to the "journey into we," or "the journey into God in the presence of others."

3. Compare your spiritual life to playing on a sports team or playing in a symphony or band. How does your private, personal practice relate to practice with the team or the orchestra?

4. Think of your faith community's liturgy in terms of a "workout of the people." What are its strengths? What are its weaknesses? How could you work to improve its effectiveness as a spiritual workout?

5. This week when you attend your faith community's gathering, notice the arrival practices, the engagement practices, the listening, response, and reentry practices. Notice how each practice affects you. Open yourself to their full impact.

6. Consider sharing this chapter with leaders in your faith community to stimulate dialogue on how your communal practices can be strengthened. Consider augmenting your weekly gatherings with special retreats for more in-depth workouts.

7. Pray for your faith community, its leaders, and the leaders, musicians, writers, architects, interior designers, janitors, hospitality workers, and others who help make gatherings possible in the via communitiva. Give thanks for them. Ask for guidance, strength, and encouragement for them. Ask also to be an answer to this prayer.

CHAPTER 12

MISSIONAL PRACTICES

The unnamed biblical writer whose words concluded the previous chapter implies that communal practices are not an end in themselves. We meet together, he says, to encourage one another and "to provoke one another to love and good deeds" (Hebrews 10:24 NRSV). In other words, when the community of faith gathers, its purpose is to equip its members for a life of love and good deeds when the community scatters.

The pastors and liturgists and worship leaders who serve the community by planning the "workout of the people" are, in this way, like aerobics instructors or sports trainers whose goal is not simply getting people to show up at the gym to work out their kinks and work up a sweat, but rather to use their time at the gym to help them live healthy, strong, productive, and athletic lives. And this is where our three types of spiritual practice come together. You could think of it like this: The practices of the contemplative way exist to prepare and equip us for community and mission (what we called the activist way earlier). The communal practices exist to prepare and equip us for contemplation and mission. The missional practices flow from our individual contemplative practices and our

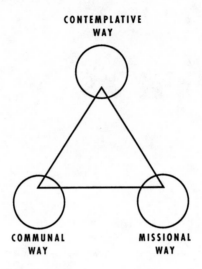

shared communal practices, and without expression in mission, our contemplative and communal practices would be incomplete and sub-Christian (or sub-Jewish or sub-Muslim). In fact, to do justice to the integral nature of the spiritual life, we have to imagine the triangle (perhaps like the Trinity itself) spinning in a dance, dynamic and expanding, never static or contracting.

In describing it this way, I'm working from an assumption that you may or may not agree with, or perhaps you've never thought about it. I'm assuming that this whole thing is not all about me. I'm assuming that the community of faith doesn't exist for me. I'm assuming that my own contemplative practices aren't ultimately about me. I'm assuming that maturity as a spiritual human being isn't complete unless it sends me out of myself into the faith community. But it's not simply about "us" either—in the sense of our church, denomination, or religion. No, I'm assuming that the faith community isn't complete unless it, in turn, is sent outside of itself into the world with saving love. In other words, I'm assuming that the church exists for the world and not the reverse—the same way that (for our purposes) yeast exists for bread or fertilizer exists for soil or light exists for darkness and not the reverse.

DOES GOD'S MISSION WORK FROM THE INDIVIDUAL TO THE WORLD, OR FROM THE WORLD TO THE INDIVIDUAL?

This assumption can be expressed as an important question: does God's mission work from the individual to the world, or from the world to the individual? Is it a part-to-whole process or a whole-to-parts process? Or put more specifically, consider two ways of thinking of spiritual formation:

A. God wants to heal the world. In order to do so, God recruits coworkers who must be healthy so they don't spread more sickness, and health care workers so they don't just keep good health to themselves. Unfortunately, there are no completely healthy people for God to work with. So in the spiritual formation process, God starts with unhealthy people and first helps them become healthier, so they can then be put to work bringing health to others, and to the world.

B. God wants to heal individuals. Individuals (we might call them "souls") are God's primary concern. If there are more and more healthy individuals, the world will become a healthier place as a by-product.

A and B are both/and approaches: they each integrate the personal and the global dimensions of faith. I would have to say that I spent the first thirty-five years following approach B, and I have since moved toward approach A for a number of reasons, foremost among which is my sense that the Bible is more global and less individualistic in its ethos, while the modern Western culture in which I was formed is the reverse. But again, either view integrates what needs to be integrated better than approaches C or D.

> C. God only cares about the world. You as an individual don't really count. Your private or personal life is your private or personal concern; just be sure you vote and work for social justice (or the spread of capitalism, communism, liberalism, or conservatism, whatever).

> D. God only cares about the individual. This whole world will soon be disposed of, so all that matters are individual souls.

The kind of integral mission or holistic spirituality that flows from the ancient way refuses C and D and chooses A and B, and my guess is that it leans toward A sooner or later. You could think of it in terms of ecology. We know that our global ecology is in trouble. The balance has been disturbed as human beings strip mountains for a layer of coal and then burn that coal so that it changes the atmosphere in ways that create unforeseen and far-reaching consequences. We build roads and parking lots and disrupt streams and wetlands and forests, and soon butterflies and turtles and salamanders and birds start disappearing. We plow fields without concern for erosion, and we plant and harvest them without concern for long-term fertility, and before long, more and more of our durable, natural wealth—to be shared by all creatures and by future generations—has been converted into short-term financial assets in somebody's bank account.

So our planetary ecology is in trouble. But isn't that outer disharmony and imbalance integrally related to the disharmony and imbalance in our inner ecology? If we are controlled by greed or fear or hate or lust internally, won't that inner ecology be expressed in the kind of world we have? If God wants the outer ecology healed, won't God necessarily want our inner ecology restored to balance and health as well? So, when we think of spiritual practices, shouldn't we think of practices that form and transform both the outer and inner ecologies of soul and world?

JESUS CALLED DISCIPLES SO HE COULD SEND THEM OUT AS APOSTLES. THEY WERE CALLED TOGETHER TO LEARN SO THEY COULD BE SENT OUT TO TEACH AND SERVE.

We could also say it like this: Jesus called disciples so he could send them out as apostles. They were called together to learn so they could be sent out to teach and serve. When a master musician invites promising young musicians to be her students, her ultimate goal is for them not to be students only, but also to become master musicians with students of their own, so the way, the tradition, of music goes on generation after generation with continuity and creativity—preserving the past but never being restricted to replaying it. Jesus calls disciples for the purpose of forming them into apostles, whom he will send out to form disciples and apostles, and so on, across all social boundaries and generations, so the "good news revolution" he launched in his little corner of the world will spread to all creation.

A well-formed disciple, then, integrates the two columns below:

PERSONAL TRANSFORMATION	FOR	GLOBAL TRANSFORMATION
DISCIPLESHIP	FOR	APOSTLESHIP
LOVE GOD	AND	LOVE NEIGHBOR AND ENEMY
GOOD HEART	FOR	GOOD WORKS
TRUST	SO AS TO	OBEY
BEING TRANSFORMED	FOR	SPREADING TRANSFORMATION
THE "INTERIOR CASTLE"	FOR	THE "KINGDOM OF GOD"
GODLINESS	FOR	OTHERLINESS

The term *otherliness* (coined by my friends Jim Henderson and Dave Richards of off-the-map.org) is really just a synonym for *love*. If the Christian faith is, as we've seen, a way, and if the way is the otherly way of love for God and for others, then what we're trying to be formed into is loving people, people who are, according to Paul in 1 Corinthians 13: "patient, kind, not envious, not boastful, not proud, not rude, not self-seeking, not easily angered, not grudge-holders, never delighting in evil, always rejoicing with truth, always protecting, always trusting (or believing the best), always hopeful, always persevering, never quitting." If our practices don't help us become people of this temper or flavor, Paul says, they're worth approximately—no, precisely—*zilch*.

That's why, when we think of spiritual practices, I believe we need to integrate the classic contemplative and communal practices with missional ones, the practices of the *via activa* that put love into action, like these:

- Forgiving those who wrong us
- Showing hospitality to strangers—or "the other"
- Praying for the sick
- Not judging but showing mercy and compassion
- Confronting evil, seeking to overcome it with good
- Serving
- Listening
- Associating with the lowly
- Giving "the holy kiss" or "eating with sinners"
- Speaking truth in love
- Practicing neighborliness, including toward enemies
- Preferring the poor rather than showing favoritism to the rich
- Speaking and working for justice
- Proclaiming the good news in word and deed
- Giving to the poor
- Throwing parties for poor and forgotten
- Walking to the other side of the street to serve those in need
- Showing empathy

In this light, Jesus' famous parable of the good Samaritan (in Luke 10) demonstrates the way that the contemplative and communal practices of the priest and Levite do not, in God's eyes, in any way substitute for the missional practices of the Samaritan. Similarly, Jesus says that a personal practice like tithing is important (Matthew 23:23; Luke 11:42), but not to the neglect of a missional practice like seeking justice, which he calls a "weightier matter." The profound integration of personal and social practices—both of which, for Jesus, are truly spiritual—could be seen as one of the hallmarks of his whole life and ministry.

In this way, Jesus is carrying on the prophetic tradition that runs deeply in Judaism. Religious people can boast of their correctness or even extravagance in the contemplative and communal practices—as seen, for example, in Isaiah 1:11–15. But all of this elicits in God, the prophet Isaiah says, something between boredom and nausea, because God wants the people to "cease to do evil, learn to do good; seek justice, rescue the oppressed, defend the orphan, plead for the widow" (Isaiah 1:16–17 NASB). They can "practice righteousness" through rigorous fasting with a long face, robed in sackcloth and ashes (Isaiah 58), but God is unimpressed. God wants the people to stop oppressing workers, stop fighting, stop pointing the finger, and stop being preoccupied with their own personal interests. God wants them to loose the bonds of injustice, break every yoke of oppression, share their bread with the hungry, invite the homeless poor into their own homes, clothe the naked, and see one another as family.

The prophet Micah echoes Isaiah's sentiments, and he concludes:

> [God] has told you, O mortal, what is good;
> and what does the Lord require of you
> but to do justice, and to love kindness,
> and to walk humbly with God? (6:8 NRSV)

All religious people agree, it seems, that we should walk humbly with God, which is the focus of many of our contemplative and communal practices. But the prophets call us further. We must show kindness, and more, we must do justice—meaning we must address the sick societal structures that keep plunging people into conditions where they will die without the kindness and compassion of others.

My friend Jim Wallis puts it memorably. We are walking—humbly, prayerfully, contemplatively, with God—down a road by the river. Then we hear someone screaming for help, caught in the current. We wade out to rescue him. Now we have shown kindness. Then we hear more screams and pull out a few more drowning people, each time showing more kindness. Eventually, as a crowd gathers and more and more screams for help fill the air, we need to say, "Quick! A bunch of us need to go upstream and find out who's pushing people into the river and stop them!" That's doing justice.[1] If we weren't walking humbly with God, perhaps we wouldn't have the courage and compassion to wade into the river on behalf of a stranger. If we didn't get wet in kindness, we wouldn't understand the urgency of justice. The three elements are inseparable, as are the contemplative way, the communal way, and the missional way. Without all three angles, our spirituality is flat-lined and dead.

SPIRITUAL EXERCISES

1. Go over the triangle diagram. How does it help you picture a dynamic spiritual life? What would be lost if any one of the angles were removed?
2. Reflect on the part-to-whole and whole-to-part approaches to God's mission. Which comes more naturally to you? What does each approach bring to the table?
3. Review the idea of discipleship for apostleship. Is this a new idea to you? How do you respond to it?
4. How does the term *otherliness* strike you?
5. Relate the practice of walking humbly with God to the practice of kindness, and relate each of them to the practice of justice.
6. Review the list of missional practices. Reflect on your experience

with each. How were you taught about these practices? How do they compare to the contemplative and communal practices?

7. Write or speak aloud a prayer in response to this chapter. In particular, talk to God about your role as disciple—one called to learn—and apostle—one sent to serve in word and deed.

CHAPTER 13

THE CYCLE WE FIND OURSELVES IN

You can construct a great way . . . a path, a road, a hallway, a passage
. . . but unless it leads to the right destination, what good is it? A few
years ago I met a missionary disillusioned by this question after three
decades of sacrificial and faithful ministry in a developing nation.

"We achieved every goal we set out to achieve," he said. When
he and his wife had first arrived, there were few churches, no major
seminaries, no Christian media, and a low percentage of Protestant
Christians. When he retired, Protestants were in the majority,
churches were multiplying at an amazing rate, many seminaries had
developed, and there were many Christian radio stations, TV programs, and bookstores. But there were realities that contradicted
that scenario of success.

"Meanwhile," he said, "every indicator of social health has
plummeted. HIV/AIDS is running rampant. Unemployment and
corruption are the norm. The sex industry is exploding. Poverty has
skyrocketed. Tribal distrust and hatred simmer beneath the surface
of every intertribal social grouping. The cities are filthy and crime-
ridden, and the countryside has suffered as people have abandoned
their farms for city life. The land itself is uglier than it was when we

came. So," he said, looking down at his hands in a kind of mournful way, "I didn't retire with a great sense of satisfaction. I feel we climbed the ladder to the top, but the ladder was leaning against the wrong building."

A Jewish chemist named Michael Polanyi (1871–1976) had a similar realization. He was Hungarian by birth but worked in Berlin, teaching at the Kaiser Wilhelm Institute for Fiber Chemistry and doing research that made him a Nobel Prize contender in two different fields of study. (His son, John, went on to win the Nobel Prize in chemistry.) Polanyi escaped Germany for England just in time to avoid being herded into the ghettos and concentration camps under Hitler. No wonder that after the war, when news of Hitler's atrocities began to leak out, Polanyi found it hard to return to science as usual.

Germany had been the poster nation of post-Enlightenment Europe, and Berlin was at or near the epicenter for everything progressive and advanced. Along with many other European intellectuals in the postwar years, Polanyi was haunted by questions like these: *How could Germany, of all places, have become what it became under Hitler? How could the most advanced nation in the most advanced continent in the most advanced century in the history of history stoop to such barbarism?* Something was lacking in the West's single-minded pursuit of reason. What was it?

Polanyi's pursuit took him to unlikely places. Instead of working with instruments and test tubes in a laboratory, he found himself consorting with artisans—wine connoisseurs, musicians, leather tanners. What especially interested Polanyi was the way in which they acquired what Polanyi came to call "personal knowledge" of their crafts. It couldn't be memorized from a book or gained from a lecture. It required the kind of knowledge an apprentice gained working elbow to elbow with the master.

This "elbow knowledge" was qualitatively different from that promoted by the modern educational system of prewar Germany. That system had spawned plenty of graduates who could get straight A's in civil engineering, but it hadn't produced enough people who would refuse to use their skills to design the ovens of Dachau. It could give people objective knowledge—say, of medicine or military strategy—but it couldn't give them the personal knowledge that would oppose "the final solution" as barbaric and evil. It could teach people genetics and eugenics, but it couldn't teach people to taste or smell when eugenics was crossing over into genocide. Distinguishing military strategy from Holocaust planning was a matter of intuitive discernment. Without such discernment, Polanyi's beloved Germany had become scientifically brilliant but morally bankrupt.

The first time I read Polanyi's masterpiece *Personal Knowledge,* I remember feeling a chill as I read the words "practical wisdom is more truly embodied in action than expressed in rules of action."[1] As a pastor, I wondered if our Christian seminaries and churches and media empires (or "ministries") had been subconsciously converted by the modern Enlightenment mind-set, just as Germany had been in the 1930s. I wondered to what degree we had come to value "rules of action"—the kinds of propositions and mandates that can be codified in books and lectures—over "practical wisdom . . . embodied in action" and carried on through traditions or communities of practice. Perhaps the art of living in the way of Jesus was no longer carried on in a holistic way by any single tradition. Perhaps we successfully climbed a ladder leaning against the wrong building, developing effective systems to teach "rules of action," but meanwhile we forgot about forming vibrant communities that preserve an art by embodying its practices through apprenticeship, elbow to elbow, generation after generation.

If that's the case, it would help explain why more and more

people in the Western world are dropping out of churches, and why after doing so, many of them report themselves happier, healthier, and closer to God and their neighbors than before.[2] What they are telling us (among other things) by their departure is that when we lose our way—when we go flat from losing the three-dimensional practice of contemplation, community, and mission we considered in the previous chapters—then we'll lose our next generation, and perhaps, after a few generations, we'll face extinction. And if by that time we've failed to wake up and find our way again, then our extinction will be no great loss and perhaps will make way for better "spiritual gene pools" to thrive, carrying on God's work.

> WHEN WE LOSE OUR WAY . . .
> THEN WE'LL LOSE OUR NEXT
> GENERATION, AND PERHAPS,
> AFTER A FEW GENERATIONS,
> WE'LL FACE EXTINCTION.

The rising numbers of church dropouts don't want to be part of a flat spiritual malformation community. In a sense, they agree with the apostles Paul and James, whom we quoted earlier: it's simply better for aspiring disciples not to gather with those who have lost their way, because by joining them and unconsciously learning from their misguided example, aspiring disciples learn malpractices that take them further and further from the way of Jesus Christ.

The histories of most of our denominations and renewal movements reflect a predictable cycle in this regard. The cycle can begin on any one of three interrelated levels and quickly spread to the others. First, there can be a problem on the level of good and right views or understanding, creating a crisis of *orthodoxy*. Perhaps a group subconsciously absorbs some bad ideas from its surrounding culture, or perhaps some bad ideas spring up from within the group itself—as anti-Semitism and white or Arab supremacy have no doubt done in Christian and Muslim history, for example. Perhaps in times of war, the community falls into what some have called a *warrior trance*, which prompts them to exaggerate their understanding of their virtues and their enemies' vices, leading to a "God loves us but hates you" mentality or worldview.

Before long, this unorthodoxy is seen and defended as orthodoxy, a condition labeled by the prophets as spiritual blindness. As a result, the group experiences "hardening of the categories," lapsing into a predictable mania for boundary maintenance, witch hunts and inquisitions, and so on. When would-be reformers arise, they are rejected as heretics, turncoats, troublemakers, disturbers of the peace, traitors, and enemies. Rhetoric heats up, logic falls victim to the rhetorical fever, and hysteria turns the group delusional and sometimes dangerous. Instead of practicing reconciliation, it practices vilification. Instead of practicing healing, it practices attack and defense. Instead of practicing concern for the other, it practices suspicion of the other. Instead of seeing itself as existing on behalf of the world, it sees itself as chosen by God to the exclusion of the world, lapsing into what missiologist Leslie Newbigin said is the greatest heresy in the history of monotheism.

By this time, the faith community has lost not only the good and right views and understandings of orthodoxy but also the good and right actions and practices of *orthopraxy*. And no doubt it has lost a good and right state of being and feeling, what some call *orthopathy*. The faith community is no longer characterized by love, joy, peace, patience, kindness, goodness, faithfulness, gentleness, and self-control, but by their opposites: hatred, fear, fury, intolerance, mean-spiritedness, constriction, rigidity, cruelty, and reactivity. In thought and word, in deed, and in spirit, the faith community has lost its way and become a school not of integrated orthodoxy, orthopraxy, and orthopathy, but of fragmenting heterodoxy, heteropraxy, and heteropathy.

But again, this process is being detailed and lamented by so many articulate voices from so many sectors of Christendom that it is probably best for us to turn from diagnosis to prescription as soon as possible. And when we do so, one painful but important group of questions predictably comes up. I hear it almost everywhere I travel around the world, in public lectures, in small-group dialogues, and in private conversations: *How do we break the cycle into which we've fallen? Is it better to try to reform our existing faith communities that have lost their way, or simply to leave and start new ones? Do we work for reformation and renewal on the one hand, or for revolution and refounding on the other?*

IS IT BETTER TO TRY TO REFORM OUR EXISTING FAITH COMMUNITIES THAT HAVE LOST THEIR WAY, OR SIMPLY TO LEAVE AND START NEW ONES?

My answer, as you might expect, is *both.*

For example, when I study the Roman Catholic Church through its history, I see the ways it has at some points rejected calls for renewal and reformation and at others welcomed them. Some, like Benedict and Francis, were welcomed as reformers. Others, like Galileo and Luther, were rejected as heretics. In some cases (as with the base community movements in Latin America, the work of Jon Sobrino and Leonardo

Boff, and perhaps with Vatican II), the church has vacillated, at first accepting renewal movements, then resisting or marginalizing them.

Protestants have a similar mixed record. For example, nearly all Protestant denominations initially rejected the more radical insights and practices of the Anabaptists or the Plymouth Brethren or the abolitionists or the Pentecostals, but over time they softened to at least some of them. The Anglicans were able to contain the renewal movement of the Wesleyans for a while, but then they ejected their more "enthusiastic" brothers and sisters.

Sometimes, what appears to be initial acceptance of a renewal movement actually becomes a kind of absorption, where the denomination domesticates, dominates, contains, and neutralizes the renewal movement that it embraces. This seems to have happened in large part to the Jesus Movement of which I was a part in the 1970s. The profound theological and missiological issues that were simmering just under the surface in those years were marginalized, while more superficial elements—like the use of guitars and drums in worship, or the relaxing of the dress code to include jeans and sports shirts alongside suits and ties—were accepted. Some people feel that something similar happened with the charismatic movement in the Roman Catholic Church.

Those unwilling or unable to be silenced, domesticated, or marginalized are thus forced to engage in dramatic revolution rather than the gradual evolution of renewal and reform. They launch new churches, new denominations, or new movements to let their more radical visions take flight. By getting distance from the groups that are not ready for them, they get space and time to experiment, learn, fail, and learn some more. Eventually, some of their experiments prove healthy and viable, and before long, the very group that rejected the reformers starts learning from them.

But meanwhile—this is so predictable and universal that I can't think of a single exception—the very zeal that propelled the rejected-reformers-turned-revolutionaries to bold innovation wears out, and their courage hardens into pride and defensiveness that renders them invulnerable to the next wave of reformation and renewal. They become exactly what they reacted against.

This is terribly depressing, so depressing that I'm tempted to move quickly to a note of hope. But I think that would be a mistake. Because unless we are sufficiently frustrated with this cycle, we won't break free from it. And we need to break free from it.

SPIRITUAL EXERCISES

1. The chapter begins with a discussion of church dropouts. Are you one? Almost? Do you know some? Schedule a gathering or dinner with church dropouts to discuss what went wrong for them and what could go right in the future.
2. Review the three orthos described in this chapter (orthodoxy, orthopraxy, orthopathy). Evaluate yourself and your faith community in light of each.
3. The story of the Holocaust is so horrific that we may fail to see the less extreme ways we, in our culture today, may be following similar paths. How can you imagine your nation, your political party, even your denomination or church somehow carrying on "the rules of the art" while missing the personal knowledge that can only come through "elbow knowledge"?
4. What advice would you give to a religious person who realized his or her religion had lost its way? Turn this advice for someone else into a prayer for yourself, and for us.

C H A P T E R 1 4

MOVING ON

There is hope. It comes when we ascend to a higher altitude and look at the bigger picture over longer spans of time. When we indulge in the art of the long view, a beautiful, higher-order pattern emerges from the messy chaos of reaction and counterreaction, renewal and retrenchment, reformation and counterreformation. Although both existing communities and new communities appear to fail when viewed from one altitude, if we move higher we see that success happens to them both, like it or not. Consider the following examples.

Galileo was silenced by an agency within the Catholic Church in 1605, which could be seen as a failure of the Church to learn or a failure of Galileo to teach, or both. But this agency of the Catholic Church was unable to stop the advance of Catholic people who simply ignored her astronomical backwardness. They looked through telescopes anyway and thought new thoughts anyway and advanced the new scientific worldview anyway. Many of these people left active involvement in the Catholic Church altogether, getting the message that their scientific endeavors were not welcome or wanted within it. Others stayed within the Church, even though some of her top officials were obviously (and for many years, un-repentantly) wrong about the structure of the universe (hardly a trivial matter, you must agree). Gradually, imperceptibly, she changed, but it took a long while to admit it: Galileo was long dead by the time the Church admitted her mistake. She changed because the center of gravity of her constituents gradually changed through influences outside the Roman Catholic Church, and when the center had shifted sufficiently, it was effortless for the ecclesiastical structures to adapt because the Catholic Church was simply catching up to where her Catholic people already were.

We might picture this process through the following diagram. In the seventeenth century, we have Catholic (A), Lutheran (B), and Reformed (C) church structures, all of which rejected Galileo's new ideas about the universe. As a result, those who agree with Galileo migrate into a new space . . . we'll call it "X," representing in this case what we call today "the scientific community." X has marginal participation from all three church bodies, but it isn't under the control of any of them. So when the institution of the church silences Galileo and rejects his insights, research into the revolution of the heavenly bodies doesn't stop; it just shifts to this new, safe space. It could even be said that the institution's rejection contributes to the development of this safe space. It progresses farther and faster than it would have if it had been sanctioned by the institution.

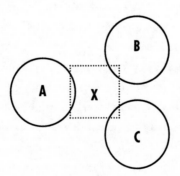

Over time, more and more participants are attracted to this safe space, and eventually its area of influence includes more and more territory within each of the church structures. The forces of growth and renewal that the institution rejects find safe space to grow outside its borders and eventually brings its resources to the institutions that rejected it.

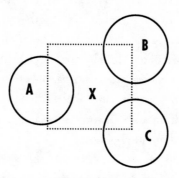

So, in this light, perhaps it was her obvious mistreatment of Galileo that helped humble the Catholic Church so she would respond less reactively to Charles Darwin 254 years later. Today, Catholic theologians like John Haught (continuing the legacy of Jesuit Pierre Teilhard de Chardin before him) are leading the way in providing exactly the kind of theological reflection on evolution that should have come alongside Galileo. Sadly, during the last century, conservative Protestants have repeated their Catholic sibling's earlier mistakes. But over time, what they reject will find or create safe space outside their borders and become a resource so that many if not most of the grandchildren of today's fundamentalists will learn and grow and move on from the misguided battles of their forebears, just as the Catholic Church did.

Or consider how the slave trade was vigorously defended by the

Anglican Church in England in the eighteenth century. A small group of Anglican friends who dared to differ from the church's official position found one another in the 1780s and early 1790s. There was James Ramsay, a navy surgeon whose duties took him to the Caribbean and onto slave ships, where he saw slavery's horrors firsthand. He eventually became an Anglican priest and antislavery activist and author. There was firebrand Thomas Clarkson, an ambitious young man who wanted to win a rhetorical contest, and whose research to prepare for the assigned question—on slavery—changed the direction of his life. There was an aspiring young politician named William Wilberforce, who was only in his early twenties when he was elected to parliament. When he changed from a skeptical nominal Anglican to a committed evangelical Anglican, he became impassioned about abolition.

These men became part of a circle of friends that was forming around the dinner table of Margaret Middleton, wife of a naval officer named Charles Middleton. She was a consummate networker, an undervalued hero in Christian history. This circle became safe space to think, dream, and conspire for justice regarding the slave trade. Their little circle connected with a larger circle of Quakers who had heard God call them, in a time of contemplative silence, to oppose slavery. Additional encouragement also came from early Methodists, including John Wesley himself. Their fledgling movement grew in the spaces between the institutional structures of their day, not within the structures themselves.

Eventually they were joined by a former slave, Olaudah Equiano, and their ranks continued to expand. Together this ecumenical and now interracial group of friends dared to defy the religious and political defenses of the slave economy and changed history. They organized boycotts and public demonstrations (which should properly be seen, I would suggest, as missional spiritual practices). They published books, spoke up everywhere they could, and networked widely with all who shared their dream. It took twenty years, but eventually they won the day. The Anglican Church and other institutional churches changed when their center of gravity shifted, and this shift occurred through forces that developed outside the boundaries of the institutions themselves.

Similarly, in the United States, most churches (excepting the Quakers, or Friends) opposed abolition and vigorously—one might say *religiously*—defended slavery as being God-ordained. After Great Britain outlawed the slave trade in 1807, the proslavery majority used every means available to defend the slave-based American economy from this liberalizing European tendency. As the Civil War broke out, denominations split over the issue of slavery, with Northern and Southern Presbyterians and Northern and Southern Baptists falling on opposite sides of the controversy. Eventually, everyone agreed that abolition was right and slavery was wrong, although it took an embarrassingly long time for this to be publicly acknowledged in some cases. The

WHERE WAS THE HOLY SPIRIT AT WORK, OUTSIDE THE RELIGIOUS INSTITUTIONS OR INSIDE THEM?

change in the churches came, again, through a gradual social process that was bigger than any church body, through networks that developed between the institutions, not within them. Through that social movement, the center of gravity shifted in the culture at large and brought the church institutions along with it.

The logical question arises: where was the Holy Spirit at work, outside the religious institutions or inside them?

The answer is, once again, both. When those inside the church structures got in the way of truth or justice or compassion, the Holy Spirit simply overflowed the old wineskins and worked beyond existing structures. But over time, the churches softened and learned, and the Holy Spirit didn't hold a grudge against them but continued graciously leading and teaching them. So God was at work with Galileo—not just the office of the Inquisition. But when the office of the Inquisition opposed the truth that Galileo told, God didn't take sides for Galileo and against the Catholic Church: God was faithful to them both and pleased whenever either side kept moving forward in truth and justice and love.

WHEN ANY SECTOR OF THE CHURCH STOPS LEARNING, GOD SIMPLY OVERFLOWS THE STRUCTURES THAT ARE IN THE WAY AND WORKS OUTSIDE THEM WITH THOSE WILLING TO LEARN.

And God was at work with Margaret Middleton, James Ramsay, William Wilberforce, and Olaudah Equiano, who opposed slavery, and God was at work with the archbishop and William Gladstone, who defended it. God was at work with the Northern Baptists and Presbyterians who dared to differ from their Southern brothers and sisters, and God was at work in the South too. And again, when the dust settled, the very institutions that opposed truth and justice and love came around to it. Hundreds of other stories—from the work of Martin Luther to the work of Martin Luther King Jr.—exemplify the same pattern.

Which brings a tremendously important lesson for us. When

any sector of the church stops learning, God simply overflows the structures that are in the way and works outside them with those willing to learn. As the old hymn says, God's truth keeps marching on. God can't be contained by the structures that claim to serve him but often try to manage and control him.

But then, as soon as the center of gravity shifts and those within the structures are ready to learn again, the Holy Spirit is there, ready to move to the next lesson in the ongoing educational process called history. Again and again through history, although we want to create "right people" and "wrong people" columns into which groups are sorted, God flips the script and sees two rows that cut across both columns: the "proud and unteachable people" row on top and the "humble and teachable people" row on the bottom. Grace flows downward, Scripture tells us, in both columns.

I find this delightful, because it tells the traditionalists that their tradition doesn't protect them from losing their way, and it tells the revolutionaries that their zeal and courage don't provide guarantees either. It calls everyone to humility and teachability, and invites everyone to climb up to a higher altitude and look for the larger pattern of God for which God constantly works—the common good.

And this, of course, is essential to finding our way. Practices are not for know-it-alls. Practices are for those who feel the need for change, growth, development, learning. Practices are for disciples. We could say that rituals are practices of learners, and ritualism is the continuation of the practice by people who have stopped learning. Similarly, we could say that traditions are the heritage of a community of learners, and traditionalism is the continuation of the heritage by people who have stopped learning.

The life-and-death question for each of our churches and denominations may boil down to this: are we a club for the elite who pretend to have arrived or a school for disciples who are still on the way?

What might happen if we experienced a conversion so that our churches became learning communities, schools of Christian practice, bands of disciples once again? How much are we willing to let go of, to let change, in order for us to leave our comfortable status quo and find our way again?

HOW MUCH ARE WE WILLING TO LET GO OF, TO LET CHANGE, IN ORDER FOR US TO LEAVE OUR COMFORTABLE STATUS QUO AND FIND OUR WAY AGAIN?

Phyllis Tickle, the general editor for the series this book introduces, offers a beautiful diagram to picture how this is happening. She creates four quadrants to illustrate four sectors of the church today. In each corner is a triangle of space for the people in that quadrant who want as much distance as possible from people in the other quadrants: charismatics who get nervous around social activists and liturgical folk, for example, and liturgical Christians who steer clear of evangelicals and social activists, and so on.

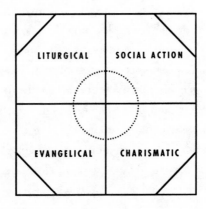

What happens when an evangelical doesn't want to leave his heritage and move to another quadrant, but he does want to learn some of the practices of the other quadrants? What happens when a charismatic gains a passion for social action and wants to learn its practices—but not by rejecting or leaving his charismatic heritage? What happens when a socially active Christian wants to go deeper in the Bible, or to experience more powerfully the Holy Spirit, or to experience liturgical worship—not in repudiation of her commitment to justice, but in order to sustain and enrich that commitment? Each of these people will move toward the circle in the center, and there they can find people willing to share their treasures and receive new treasures too.[1]

TRYING TO STOP PEOPLE FROM LEARNING, SHARING, AND LOVING IS A LOSING GAME BECAUSE IT MEANS WORKING AGAINST GOD AND THE PLOTLINE OF GOD'S UNIVERSE.

At the center, safe space happens. A learning community forms. New possibilites emerge. A new day dawns. If the guardians of our fragmented religious institutions forbid their members to meet in the center, the members will not be able to comply. They will simply go undercover and arrange secret liaisons, because what they need is not contained within their own quadrant.

Eventually, the shared resources, vitality, and new possibilities that unfold in the center will penetrate and reinvigorate all four quadrants, maybe even reaching the outer four corners too. Trying to stop people from learning, sharing, and loving is a losing game because it means working against God and the plotline of God's universe.

SPIRITUAL EXERCISES

1. The author promises hope in this chapter. Did the chapter fulfill the promise for you? Why or why not?

2. Recount the stories told in the chapter—of Galileo, of abolition, of evolution. How are they similar? What can you learn from each?

3. Reflect on the term *safe space*. Where have you found safe space in your spiritual journey? Do you know people who need some safe space now? How could you be part of creating that safe space? What ideas are considered dangerous in your context, requiring safe space to consider them? Who might consider this book dangerous, and why?

4. Picture ways that the Holy Spirit might be overflowing inflexible or unteachable structures in our churches today.

5. Both traditionalists and revolutionaries can be proud and unteachable. Explain how. Both can be humble and teachable as well. Explain how.

6. Turn this chapter into a prayer, first for the church or movement of which you are part, and especially its leaders, and second for yourself and your role in that church or movement, and third for people working to create safe spaces that can become seedbeds for renewal.

PART 3
ANCIENT

CHAPTER 15

PRACTICING THE ANCIENT WAY

I love fishing. It doesn't matter what kind. I can be sitting on a dock with a cane pole, catching perky bluegills and sunfish, or plopping lures in front of largemouth bass from a kayak or canoe. I can be standing waist-deep in the Potomac River, watching freshly hooked smallmouth bass hurl themselves into the great above, or sitting on the sand at sunrise beside a tall rod with line cast beyond the crashing surf. There's something about fishing I've enjoyed since I was a boy learning the practice from my grandmother—a kind and proper lady who wore a dress while fishing and threaded her own night crawlers on the hook and never seemed happier than when she was sitting in a rowboat, waiting for a nibble.

You learn a lot of other things accidentally while you learn to fish, and most anglers would agree that there's not much more to fishing than learning. The fish are teaching you by what they bite and what they reject. The weather is teaching you. The insects are teaching you. Your fellow anglers are teaching you (in between lying to you about the size of their last catch). I find it interesting that Jesus hung out with fishermen and compared his school of spiritual practice to the school of fishing, which for them was a matter of nets rather than rods and reels. He basically called his "kingdom of God" project another form of fishing: learning to bring human beings into a new network, you might say.

I've been fishing for about forty-five years, but I'm newer to fly-fishing. In my travels over the last year, I happened to meet some expert fly fishermen, one in South Africa and two in the Rocky Mountains of the United States, who offered to be my guide and introduce me to their waters and maybe a few fish too. I was fishing a pool with one of them who was watching my form from under a nearby tree. He didn't know I could overhear him and his buddy talking. "What do you think?" the buddy asked. "Is he any good?"

"He's obviously done this before," my guide replied.

His halfhearted endorsement of my skill made me a bit self-conscious, and in my next back-cast I managed to hook a branch of the tree they were sitting under. After a few minutes of retrieving the fly and disentangling my line, I set up again, a bit humiliated, not knowing that things were about to get worse. In my next cast, after a few graceful back-casts to reestablish my rhythm and get some distance, something happened, and suddenly I felt like a criminal being captured by Spiderman as a web of line fell down on me.

My guide slowly got up and approached me. "You know, you've got a pretty good cast. All the right elements are there. But if you don't mind, I can show you three things that help a lot of fly fishermen improve their form." And he did, and on my more recent trip, I received a few more tips. My education continues.

If you want to learn fly-fishing, there is a worldwide community of anglers who carry on the tradition, the way of fishing for trout or salmon or char or whatever. (I was surprised to learn that South African anglers fly-fish for carp, a fact I'm including for no other reason than the fact that I think other anglers will want to know.) If you want to learn golf, there is a worldwide golf community, and the same for shape-note singing and knitting and quilting and wooden boat making and Italian cooking and basically everything.

And this is what I think our churches (or faith communities by whatever name) are meant to be, and can be, and sometimes are. When our churches are schools of practice, they make—and change—history. Otherwise, they simply write history and argue about it, and of course, in so doing they tend to repeat it.

The New Testament ex- emplifies this pattern. The Gospels weren't written until decades after the events they described transpired—per- haps because Jesus created such vitality and foment that it took decades for anyone to have time to catch their breath and write down what had gone on. Similarly, the

WHEN OUR CHURCHES ARE SCHOOLS OF PRACTICE, THEY MAKE— AND CHANGE—HISTORY.

Epistles are hardly histories of the early church, but rather are literary artifacts of the early church, most of them written by a fellow who was constantly on the move and couldn't slow down enough to write until he got shipwrecked for the winter or thrown into jail. There's a breathlessness about the whole affair, from Matthew to Revelation, and the same could be said of Genesis to Malachi too.

How different is a breathless, history-changing learning com- munity from a placid or contentious panel of scholars and experts who are less interested in learning anything than they are in defend- ing what they already think they know and attacking what other experts think they know. The former group is on its way, journey- ing, and the latter is by the way, critiquing.

Of course, I'm not saying any of this to denigrate the importance of studying history. The opposite, in fact, because when the community of faith realizes it has lost its way, it begins moving forward by looking back—not to congratulate itself, not to defend itself, not to celebrate itself, but to critique itself and determine the trajectory it used to be on in better days. It looks to its ancient practices to help it reset its future course.

When we look back today, back before the twentieth century, back before the Protestant and Catholic missionary eras, back before the Reformation, back before the Great Schism, we find that what became the Western church and what became the Eastern church shared a common ancient treasure—a description of the Christian life as a life on the way. Today, reflective scholars, such as William Fowler and others, have created useful and helpful typologies of the spiritual life, showing predictable phases or stages or seasons of spiritual development. The ancient church also had a schema to describe the spiritual path, and it consisted of three phases known as "the threefold way." I'm all for new and fresh schemas to describe the way of faith; in fact, I've tried my hand at creating a schema of my own.[1] But I am also all for looking back to see what we used to know and may have forgotten.

The threefold way can be described as stages, but to do so would be misleading, because one doesn't complete one stage and

> **WHEN THE COMMUNITY OF FAITH REALIZES IT HAS LOST ITS WAY, IT BEGINS MOVING FORWARD BY LOOKING BACK.**

move to the next. It would be more accurate to describe the three-fold way as three dimensions or emphases or zones of the spiritual life. One learns these dimensions or emphases or zones in a given order, and each new dimension presupposes the continuation of what has come before. The first two dimensions find fulfillment in the third. Each has two names, one from the Western church (in Latin) and one from the Eastern church (in Greek).

The *Via Purgativa* or *Katharsis*. First is the dimension of self-examination in which we discover the prevalence and power and intensity of the evil that already lies within us like viruses in software. This self-examination leads us to seek to be purified, purged, debugged, liberated, and transformed.

The *Via Illuminativa* or *Fotosis*. Then comes the dimension of enlightenment, receiving the light of God's truth and character and vigor and love into our lives. If katharsis is like the removing of clouds so the sun can shine through, fotosis is sunbathing, exposing our souls to God's light so we can flourish like a tree, humming with photosynthesis. We grow robust with life and bountiful with fruit. Fotosis means having our minds and imaginations enlightened and our hearts and energies warmed with the light of God.

The *Via Unitiva* or *Theosis*. Then we come to unification of our being with God, so that we are taken into God and God fills us. In this process, our will becomes increasingly one with God's will, our emotions with God's emotions, our thoughts with God's thoughts, and our words and actions with God's words and actions. Our individuality isn't obliterated through this union, but rather made sacred and in this way enhanced. By being harmonized with God, we also become harmonized with everything else that is harmonized with God. In musical terms, we come to resonate to God's frequency, or to reverse a medical term, we become thoroughly infected with a "strong case of God," which is what *theosis* sounds like to me: a healthy disease we catch from God.

The seven ancient practices come together in the ancient threefold way. Fasting, pilgrimage, common daily prayers, a weekly day of rest, annual holy days and seasons, tithing, and the sacred meal find their fulfillment in the ways they contribute to our purgation, illumination, and union with God.

> THE SEVEN ANCIENT PRACTICES COME TOGETHER IN THE ANCIENT THREEFOLD WAY.

Perhaps you can best proceed by imagining yourself to be a young spiritual seeker who has just come into possession of a time machine. You have gone back to the Middle Ages on a spiritual quest. You wander through the land, hungry and thirsty to discover your purpose and fulfill your potential in God's world. You come to a monastery and are given a hospitable welcome. You meet with the abbess, a short, wrinkled, slightly hunched-over woman who walks with a stick at a pace that exceeds the speed limit you would imagine for a wrinkled, slightly hunched-over woman. You'll explain that you have lost your way, and you now seek to learn the ancient way if her community is willing to share it with you. She invites you in for lunch and tells you over a simple meal that you must begin with the via purgativa or katharsis.[2]

SPIRITUAL EXERCISES

1. The author describes his love of fishing in the tradition of anglers. What is something you love? Share your experiences in that tradition.

2. Describe a faith community that is "on the way," in contrast to one that is "by the way."

3. Review the threefold way that comes from the shared tradition of East and West.

4. The author is trying to stir anticipation and curiosity about the threefold way. What questions do you have? What more do you want to learn?

5. Turn your curiosity and questions into a prayer.

CHAPTER 16

KATHARSIS (VIA PURGATIVA)

"The *via purgativa* in the Latin of the West or *katharsis* in the Greek of the East," the abbess explains, "is the gate through which we enter the ancient way and its practices." She then offers you an analogy. If the soul is a house that has fallen into disrepair, she says, or perhaps a house that was abandoned and boarded up before it was completed, you must begin by purging the house of the trash, dirt, and vermin that have accumulated within it.

So the purgative way first instructs you to take the boards off the windows and tear down the heavy old curtains that hide or obscure the mess inside. Then it tells you that you must take some soap and water and scrub the windows of their grime. As you begin the reclamation, everything depends on letting light come in, because without light you won't be able to see what's dirty and what needs to be cleaned and repaired, she explains.

She says that the ancient saints have identified three things that obstruct light from entering the soul: First is pride, the abbess explains, a preoccupation with oneself and one's power. Second is lust, a preoccupation with pleasure in general and sexual pleasure in particular. Third is greed, a preoccupation with money and possessions. "Pride, lust, greed . . . money, sex, and power . . . the lust of the flesh, the lust of the eyes, and the pride of life . . . however they're described," the abbess says, "unless we acknowledge their power in our lives, we won't make further progress on the ancient way. We will stay in darkness."

Then the abbess does something unexpected. She tells you there is an old cottage behind the monastery's main buildings that she would be happy for you to stay in for as long as you'd like, but it has been used as a storage shed for so long that it needs a lot of work to be made habitable. She invites you to spend the rest of the day cleaning out the old cottage so you can sleep there tonight. When you seem interested, she walks you to the far corner of the monastery and shows you around. Before she leaves, she says, "You know, our whole life in this monastery is based on katharsis. We take vows of poverty, chastity, and obedience as a way of committing ourselves to a life-long struggle with the darkness that can destroy every life. Our vow of poverty is a way for us to reject the darkness of greed, and chastity rejects lust. And by submitting ourselves to a spiritual director and the larger needs of our community, we step out of the shadows of pride. I hope you will understand why we make these vows as you share our way of life in the days ahead."

She walks back to the main building, at an amazingly spry pace—and you begin to pry off shutters and tear down old curtains. As you take stock of the spiders and mice and pigeons that have made the old cottage their home, as you encounter dust and rust and junk, as you scrub windows and build a fire to burn piles of trash and heaps of broken furniture far beyond repair, the abbess's words about the purgative way become something you can feel, see, smell, and taste. Your first night is uncomfortable because so much remains to be done before the cottage is truly habitable. With some real and even more imagined bugs creeping over you in the darkness, you sleep fitfully at best and are a bit bleary-eyed when we meet the abbess the next morning.

You talk about your experience and complain about lack of sleep. "Imagine how tired and grouchy you would be," she says with a laugh, "if you had to live in a dilapidated, filthy shack every day and never purged it of its filth! Now you see why so many people in our world are so prickly and cross and hard to get along with. They haven't had a good night's sleep in years because their souls are in such disrepair and misery." She reviews the "big three" spiritual dangers with you, the dark forces that make our souls—and our world—what they are. You reflect on the world of your time and the destructive role of money/greed, sex/lust, and power/pride within it.

And not only the world in general, but also the church in particular. You think of the ubiquitous clergy scandals of recent decades, and you realize that whatever the strengths of the seminaries, the via purgativa isn't a strong enough part of the curriculum. Arrogant and greedy televangelists, sexual abuse scandals among priests and pastors, unholy alliances between religious leaders and political parties . . . they tell you that under their vestments, within their stained-glass windows, behind the TV screens and doctrinal statements, undisturbed by their God-talk and all the other accoutrements of religious life, money, sex, and power haven't been dealt with, but have instead been too often baptized.

Now we would misunderstand katharsis if we thought that no one could graduate from this stage of the spiritual life until he or she had mastered pride/power, greed/money, and lust/sex. Nobody would ever graduate. But the ancient way challenges novices—beginners in the ancient practices—to discover the terrifying power and despicable resilience of pride, greed, and lust by confronting them. In so doing, they would also come to know the weakness of human flesh to withstand them. By facing these monsters and exposing them to the light of God, novices would not be cured of pride, greed, and lust, but they would begin to be cured of a dangerous naïveté about them.

If you popped back into your time machine and re-entered our world today, what might the via purgativa look like? How might it be practiced in Miami or Tokyo or Manhattan or Tehran?

THE ANCIENT WAY CHALLENGES NOVICES— BEGINNERS IN THE ANCIENT PRACTICES— TO DISCOVER THE TERRIFYING POWER AND DESPICABLE RESILIENCE OF PRIDE, GREED, AND LUST BY CONFRONTING THEM.

It might involve a small group or pair of spiritual friends who gather regularly—weekly, monthly, whatever—to review honestly together the hold of money, sex, and power on their lives. They might gather in a home or restaurant or online. Their gathering wouldn't be an "accountability group" exactly, where the shame of having to admit failures to your group members is supposed to motivate you to avoid failing. It would instead be a "vulnerability group," where the members tried to admit to themselves and others how much power pride, greed, and lust have on them.

They might be aided in this process through journaling, where they took time each day to write down anecdotes where the big three showed up in their thoughts, words, or behavior. Or they might take on special challenges—fastings, if you will—where they deprived themselves of things that reinforced the darkness in their souls by for-tifying pride, greed, or lust. For example, one month they might focus on pride, agreeing to go without defending themselves when-ever they are criticized, or agreeing not to tell jokes for the next week—*not* to pursue being boring and grim and dull, but to avoid being a show-off, getting laughs at the expense of others, and thus feeding pride. The purpose of doing so would *not* be so they would never be able to entertain others and bless them with the laughter that comes from a good joke, but rather the reverse: so they *could* do so, often and freely, but not driven by the prideful craving to show off.

Or more positively, they might make a pact to find someone each day to serve secretly, being sure not to get credit for a good deed. Or they might agree to spend extra time with children, the sick, the elderly, the mentally handicapped or ill, seeking to love and serve the powerless and lowly instead of seek-ing to hang out and be seen with the powerful and prestigious.

PURGATION HAS EVERYTHING TO DO WITH PRACTICE, NOT PENANCE.

Do you begin to see how purgation works? It has nothing to do with penance in the sense of paying for one's sins. Disciples understand that God forgives and saves by grace, so *paying* and *earning* aren't even part of the sane disciple's vocabulary. Purgation has everything to do with practice, not penance: practicing humil-ity and service rather than pride and power, practicing generosity and simplicity rather than greed, practicing self-control and a willingness to suffer pain for a good cause rather than a lust for pleasure and comfort.

Practitioners of the via purgativa could address greed by agreeing not to watch television or read magazines in a deliberate fast from advertising. They could conspire on a project that would require of them a greed-busting financial commitment. They could practice being extravagant tippers, extravagant in giving compliments and encouragement, extravagant in taking time with people, but not extravagant in indulging their own spending whims, thus stiff-arming greed and exercising muscles of generosity.

And practitioners of katharsis could address lust by looking at people's eyes and faces rather than . . . other body parts. They could work against the tendency to lavish attention on the physically attractive by practicing special consideration for people who are . . . otherwise. They could practice fasting from various pleasures, as one might do during Lent, for example, not because pleasure is bad—what a ridiculous thought!—but because pleasure is so good that we are all in danger of becoming addicted to it.

> THAT'S PERHAPS THE SECRET OF KATHARSIS, RIGHTLY PRACTICED: ONE THING A PERSON CANNOT BE WHEN HONESTLY FIGHTING LUST, GREED, AND PRIDE IS . . . *PROUD*, AND PRIDE, IT TURNS OUT, IS THE MOST DANGEROUS DARKNESS OF ALL.

So, far from the grim negativity we often associate with pallid, squeamish saints, these are the practices of people seeking moral virility and robust integrity, the power to say no to three of the most powerful forces in our lives: an insecure ego that needs more power and attention; an unfulfilled craving for pleasure; and the urge to reach for the credit card to acquire, accumulate, hoard, compare. People have no idea how strong a pull sex, money, and power have on them until they try to resist their pull.

And nobody who tries to resist their black-hole gravity or seductive magnetism is very successful very fast or for very long, but that's perhaps the secret of katharsis, rightly practiced: one thing a person cannot be when honestly fighting lust, greed, and pride is . . . *proud*, and pride, it turns out, is the most dangerous darkness of all.

The abbess would invite us into the life of the community in the days ahead, and somehow, the more we would face our own demons of pride, greed, and lust, the more gentle and kind we would become toward others, the less judgmental, the less harsh, the more empathetic, because we realize as never before that everyone is pitched in an invisible inner battle, and the battle isn't easy for anyone.

A child learns to walk before she learns to run, but once she learns to run, she doesn't stop walking. That's a skill she'll depend on all her life. Similarly, the disciple who learns the via purgativa and then moves on to the second and third stages of the spiritual life never stops practicing katharsis, but because she has practiced katharsis, she is now ready to move on in the ancient threefold way.

SPIRITUAL EXERCISES

1. How do you respond to the fictional character of the abbess?
2. Review the metaphor of the dilapidated shack and its cleanup and renovation.
3. What relationships can you draw from the following groups of

three: money, sex, and power; lust, pride, and greed; poverty, chastity, and obedience; and lust of the flesh, lust of the eyes, and boastful pride of life.

4. Have you ever been part of a group like the one described in this chapter, seeking purgation or katharsis? What appeals to you about this group? Does anything frighten you or push you away?

5. Imagine your life if you experienced greater purgation from greed.

6. Imagine your life if you experienced greater purgation from lust.

7. Imagine your life if you experienced greater purgation from pride.

8. Why is pride the most dangerous of all the dangers?

9. Translate your previous answers into a written or spoken-aloud prayer.

C H A P T E R   1 7

FOTOSIS (VIA ILLUMINATIVA)

Imagine that you have returned to the medieval monastery to learn about the second dimension of the threefold way. The abbess welcomes you and leads you into the garden. She points out the health of the beans and pumpkins, the squash and beets, and then she invites you to sit on a bench and begins to explain. "The via illuminativa, or the way of fotosis, means that now, having removed the boards and curtains from the long-closed windows of our souls, we learn to let light in. Light makes sight possible, and the spiritual life is, in many ways, about seeing." She might then remind you of what Jesus said in the Sermon on the Mount: the eye is the lamp of the body. If our eyes are good, our whole lives will be full of light, but if our eyes are bad, our lives will be filled with terrible darkness (Matthew 6:22–23).

"Jesus also loved to perform healings of blind people. Those miracles have a message for all of us: we, too, are blind and need to have our vision, our outlook, our perspective healed." Then she talks about how our vision of so many things is distorted, beginning with God. "Some people don't see God at all, but others are even worse off, because the God they see is a monster or a toy or a totem or a fetish."

After a long dialogue about our need for a fresh vision of God, she adds, "And we don't see ourselves correctly either. And of course, we don't see others accurately. If we could see ourselves and others through God's eyes, everything would be so different for the world."

Then she goes on to name other things we don't see clearly—money, time, possessions, illness, trials, our failures, other living creatures, the earth, the heavens, even death. She concludes with a laugh, "There really isn't anything left that we do see clearly! And the via illuminativa is all about seeing everything in the light of God."

> THE VIA ILLUMINATIVA IS ALL ABOUT SEEING EVERYTHING IN THE LIGHT OF GOD.

Then she turns your attention to the plants growing around you—pole beans creeping up a tripod of sticks, sunflowers facing east for the morning sun, pumpkin leaves as big as two hands spread out together, with softball-sized pumpkins forming beneath them—still dark green without even a hint of orange. "Living things draw all their life from the sun. If you take a plant and put it in a pot and bring it inside, within a day it begins to look sad and weak. It might feebly stretch toward the nearest window, but soon it withers and dies. That's what I think when I look in the faces of so many people. They have too little light to thrive, too little of God's light. They're hiding in the shadows, or maybe trapped, afraid to come out into the beautiful day of God."

You might reflect on a word you learned in high school to describe the movement of sunflowers and other plants toward sunlight: *heliotropism.* You would see the ancient way as a kind of "theotropism," a turning toward God's light.

The abbess continues her little sermon: "The apostle John makes a remarkable statement in his first epistle. He tells his readers that he will summarize the message—the message he and his fellow disciples received from Jesus, and the message they proclaim everywhere. 'Here it is,' he says, and wraps it up in one simple sentence: 'God is light, and in God there is no darkness at all.' Do you see?"

You might respond that if a seminary student in your day tried to sum up the Christian message in this way, he or she would probably flunk out. But devotees of the ancient threefold way love the imagery of light, so for its practitioners, there could be no better answer than John's.

This second dimension of the threefold way is about letting the light of God into our

YOU WOULD SEE THE ANCIENT WAY AS A KIND OF "THEOTROPISM," A TURNING TOWARD GOD'S LIGHT.

souls, our beings, our lives. Before katharsis, while we were still in denial about our pride, lust, and greed, we were uninterested in God's light. But now, with some awareness of how powerful and destructive these dark forces are, we want the light to penetrate us in every part of our being and drive the darkness away. So in order to let God's light into our minds, we will engage in practices of illumination, fotosis, enlightenment.

One such practice is study—study of the Bible especially, but also of other spiritual literature. Through study we welcome the light of God into our minds. But our minds are more than our intellect or our analytical apparatus. We also have our imagination, our intuitive apparatus. So we take light in through other means as well.

On the via illuminativa, we love to go to church gatherings. We are eager to sense God's light in songs and sermons. We want to see it in the faces of our pastors and fellow disciples. We want to smell it in the coffee or home-baked cookies we share, and we want to taste it in the Eucharist. When we are at home or driving in the car or sitting on a plane or train, we are eager to welcome in God's light through books, lectures, podcasts, and websites, in novels or poetry, in music and art. When we go to the movies, we aren't just seeking entertainment: as we're trained in the ancient way of fotosis, we are seeking God's enlightenment. In solitude, we recall God's light through meditation, and in conversation, we convey it to others. In a bird's song, in the night sky, in the taste of food, our souls learn to sense the light of God, and the more we see, the more we want to see.

> IN ORDER TO LET GOD'S LIGHT INTO OUR MINDS, WE WILL ENGAGE IN PRACTICES OF ILLUMINATION, FOTOSIS, ENLIGHTENMENT.

Katharsis prepares the way for fotosis. As our insatiable lust for pleasure is tamed, in its place grows something beautiful and new: a hunger and thirst for truth and justice and goodness and beauty and every pure and holy reality, like the infrared to ultraviolet spectrum that is contained in the white light of God. As we are driven less and less by pride, we stop craving to be in the spotlight, and instead we want to see everything in the light of God. We stop wanting to be stars and instead we want to see stars and savor the beauty of their light. As we are liberated from greed—the craving to accumulate things and have them in our pockets or on our portfolios or under our control—we learn the greater joy of accumulating light, of putting out our branches and leaves, so to speak, of being in the light and warmed by its power.

For God to be rendered to us as light does so much for us, and it does so beautifully. It tells us that God is, in a sense, common, ubiquitous, everywhere, every day. It tells us that God is real yet immaterial, peaceful yet dynamic, powerful yet gentle, and comprehensible yet incomprehensible. Light confounds us: is it something we see, or something by which we see everything else? How is it wave and particle and both, and how is God Father, Son, and Spirit? Light, like God, relativizes time and space and thus renders us part of something big and beautiful and fast and timeless and mysterious and wonderful and colorful and . . . spiritual.

FOR GOD TO BE RENDERED TO US AS LIGHT DOES SO MUCH FOR US, AND IT DOES SO BEAUTIFULLY.

This is the delight of the via illuminativa. Practitioners of fotosis are often supremely happy people, ecstatic as children on the first day after winter's end, when their coats and shoes can come off and they can run barefoot in the grass, joining in the awakening and enlightenment of springtime. Lengthening days mean more time, more warmth, more fun, more joy, more life.

Practitioners of fotosis are often this way, but not always, because an inescapable part of fotosis is the experience of night. One's enjoyment of the light of God is punctuated with nights and sometimes long, long nights, spiritual storms—low pressure systems, atmospheric depressions—when the clouds are thick and gray for days, weeks, months, even years. It's cold and it rains, and the memory of a summer day mocks the gloomy present like a fantasy that was never real, too good to ever be true again. One learns about light not just by being in its presence, but also by experiencing its absence. Who, after all, loves the light of day more than a person who has been trapped for days in a cave, or held hostage in a basement, or cooped up in a hospital room under fluorescent tubes whose flat artificial light insults the indescribable radiance of sun and stars? Who loves light more than a prisoner whose dreams recall the glow of trees reflected on water, the gold of a child's hair glistening, the shimmer of dew on leaf, or the glint of sweat and tears on skin?

ONE LEARNS ABOUT LIGHT NOT JUST BY BEING IN ITS PRESENCE, BUT ALSO BY EXPERIENCING ITS ABSENCE.

It's only those who have come to love the light who are devastated by its absence—the dark night of the soul, a time when light is gone. Nobody would choose this experience, but having gone fully through it and experienced its gifts, nobody would forego it. The same could not be said of those partway through the dark night; for them, it is still an unmitigated horror and travesty, an offense and wound that can't be anesthetized until it heals, in time, by the return of the light.

This light is not just something we want to see: it is luminosity so beautiful that it awakens in us something which C. S. Lewis rightly said "can hardly be put into words." We want "to be united with the beauty we see, to pass into it, to receive it into ourselves, to bathe in it, to become part of it."[1] If I call this passion for light a kind of lust, a kind of greed, a kind of longing for glory that has a certain resonance with pride, yet is its polar opposite—will I desecrate the light itself, or will I show why pride, lust, and greed must die so something greater can rise from their ashes? If I try to review some of the practices integral to fotosis, will I desecrate the light as if it is something that can be turned on by a switch? The danger is real, but I must at least try.

There's contemplation, which is a simple dwelling in the light, peaceful, silent, receptive. There's *lectio divina* or spiritual reading, where the mind receives the light of truth and the emotions receive the light of love and the will receives the light of invitation and command. There's practicing God's presence, which is simply keeping one's eyes open to the light, wherever one is, whatever one is doing. There's fellowship, where one seeks to discern the light in other people, and there's worship, where one sings and dances and simply basks in the light—like a lizard on a rock, like sunbathers at the beach, like picnickers on a summer vacation.

In the coming days, back at the monastery, you enter into the practices of fotosis with the community of faith. You gradually understand their desire to pray and read and reflect together five times a day not as a grim duty, but as a practice of the via illuminativa, keeping the individual heart and the communal spirit open to God's gracious infusion of light and grace. Just as in our day a husband and wife might call each other several times a day just to check in and say, "I love you," they wanted to check in with God and keep their hearts open to enlightenment from the Holy Spirit.

So you gradually synchronize your life to their ancient rhythm. You rise just before sunrise to pray and sing and chant or read the Scriptures—not as a grim duty, but expressing your growing desire not to miss the sunrise of God's new day by sleeping in. You gather again midmorning, at midday, at sunset, and before bedtime—and gradually come to feel this community's daily rhythm as a practice of illumination, a habit of fotosis.

After you've had some weeks to experience it and let it form you, the abbess explains to you the history and meaning of their daily rhythm, which they call the divine hours or the daily office. The term, she explains, is drawn from the Latin *opus*, meaning "work," but we might translate it slightly, recalling chapter 12, as "workout," "exercise," or "practice." It is, simply put, a practice of illumination. To pause at several fixed times each day—drawing from even more ancient Jewish practice (Psalm 119:164; Acts 3:1; 10:9)—isn't for this monastic community the interruption of more important "secular" work with less important "spiritual" work. Nor is it an escape from less important "mundane" or "profane" work to more important "holy" or "sacred" work. Rather, their daily rhythm integrates work (*labora*) with prayer (*ora*) in pursuit of a wholly holy life. The practice of fotosis, the via illuminativa, thus infuses each part of each day—waking, morning, midday, evening, bedtime—with light, the light of God.

When you take your time machine back to the present—to our world of coffee shops and shopping malls, reality TV and e-mail spam, heat pumps and water bills, vacations and overtime—you will be filled with new questions. What it will mean to practice the via illuminativa in a traffic jam? How will you bring fotosis into conference calls and conflict resolution? How can you stay open to enlightenment on the golf course or at your kids' soccer games? How will you integrate ora and labora in your jammed-tight schedule, where one day might include a business breakfast, a conference call, a sales meeting, a performance review, sixty-four urgent e-mails, a working lunch, a strategic planning meeting, editing four memos and writing an important progress report, avoiding the main highway on the way home because it's partially closed for construction, getting home late for a family dinner of store-bought pizza, rushed because you have to attend the PTA parents' night at your kids' elementary and middle schools, after which you hope to squeeze in a few minutes watching the *Colbert Report* before falling asleep just after midnight?

The challenge can be seen either as insurmountable and depressing or as unprecedented and exciting—depressing and insurmountable because today's postmodern world seems so different from the abbess's premodern world, or unprecedented and exciting because each day offers us such a variety of fascinating experiences into which the light of God can be infused. Books like the one I'm now writing and you're now reading invite us to become collaborators, coconspirators, and contributing partners in a growing, essential, fresh global conversation among people who lean away from "depressing and insurmountable" and lean toward "unprecedented and exciting."

We've seen how katharsis prepares us for fotosis. But what does fotosis prepare us for? In the Middle Ages, there was a beautiful metaphor that captured the progression from the via illuminativa to the via unitiva, from fotosis to theosis. We can imagine another visit to our favorite abbess to learn what that progression looks like.

SPIRITUAL EXERCISES

1. Respond to the abbess's statement, "The spiritual life is about seeing."

2. Talk about your experience of "theotropism."

3. Share your experiences of the absence of light during a dark night of the soul. How did these experiences seem to hurt you? Help you? If you could remove them from your life, how would you be different?

4. Review the daily rhythm of the monastery. What is attractive about this way of life? Would it be possible to integrate that rhythm into your daily life today?

5. The author invites the readers to be "collaborators, coconspirators, and contributing partners" in a shared enterprise. Describe that enterprise, and let it inspire you to pray.

6. Acquire a copy of the following songs, listen to them several times, and discuss them in relation to fotosis:
   —David Wilcox and Nance Pettit, "How Did the Rose Open," "Slicing Potatoes," and "On a Day When the Wind Is Perfect," from *Out Beyond Ideas* (davidwilcox.com, outbeyondideas.org).
   —Carrie Newcomer, "Holy as a Day is Spent," from *The Gathering of Spirits* (carrienewcomer.com).

7. If possible, take a walk in the daylight. As you walk, let light teach you about God. Ask God to help you see. Let God be your walking companion. Then, if possible, take a similar walk after sundown or before sunrise. Share what you experience on these "prayer walks."

C H A P T E R   1 8

THEOSIS (VIA UNITIVA)

It's a cool autumn evening as you enter the monastery, and the abbess invites you to sit by the crackling fire in her small but comfortable quarters. She asks you how your cottage is suiting you, and you laugh as you recall what a ramshackle mess it was just a few weeks ago. Each day you have cleaned it up a bit more, and now it has the feel of a real home. She reminds you of the ways your renovation project has been a parable of the ancient threefold way, beginning with purgation and continuing through illumination.[1] Then she walks over to the fire and picks up a rod of cold, charred iron that lies on the stone hearth. With it, she stirs the burning logs, and they crackle a bit more loudly and send up a swirling flurry of sparks.

"When a young couple builds or inherits their first home," she explains, kneeling by the fire, "the hearth is the heart of their home. To me, this is a picture of all life: the fire of God—radiating warmth and light—is the center of everything." You talk for a few minutes about the fascination of fire, thinking that before television, the dancing flames of the hearth were probably the focal point of attention for thousands of homes on thousands of nights.

Then the abbess again stirs the fire with the fireplace poker she has been holding for the last few minutes. "One of the first things a couple needs to acquire is a fireplace poker. They save up their money or some tradable goods until they can pay the local blacksmith to fashion one for them. They use it every morning to stir into flame the embers left from the previous night. They use it to position the kindling and logs they add to the fire. And of course they use it to pick up a pot by its hot handle to remove it from the fire." As she says these words, she removes a pot of boiling water, rises slowly, and shuffles across the room to make you a cup of herb tea in a flavor you've never encountered.

As you sip the tea, she points to the fire and says, "You'll notice that I made a mistake a few minutes ago. It's a common mistake that I actually did on purpose to show you something. See?" You follow her gaze and realize that she left the fireplace poker with its tip in the hottest embers. And something at once expected yet remarkable has happened: the rod has begun to glow. The tip of the rod that is deepest into the hottest embers is now indistinguishable from them: it pulses with the same orange luminosity and the same mysterious radiance. The next section of iron also glows orange, but it doesn't seem to be surrounded by the same halo of radiance. Beyond that, the next sections are white, then gray, and then the normal rough black of a normal rod of unpolished iron.

You simply stare for a few minutes, without speaking. Then she asks you, "What is my mistake teaching you?" You respond slowly, as little by little a kind of revelation strangely warms your heart.

The abbess doesn't have any understanding of atoms and molecules, of radiant energy or heat transfer, of rapid oxidation and combustion. So your observations make no sense to her at all. She kindly pushes aside your nonsense, and in her prescientific language, she instructs you about the nature of iron being cold and dark and the nature of fire being hot and light. She explains that the power of fire is far greater than the power of iron, so instead of the iron making the fire cold, the fire makes the iron hot. As a result, she says, if the iron is placed in the fire long enough, the nature of fire overshadows the nature of iron, and the iron begins to "catch" the nature of the fire. The light and heat of fire illuminate and warm the darkness and cold of iron so that the iron is fire-ized. It "partakes," she says, "in the nature of fire until it becomes light and heat itself."

She asks you to remove the fireplace poker. As you reach out to oblige, she blurts out: "No, not like that! You'll burn yourself, child!" She directs you to grab an old rag to protect your hands. After you remove the poker, you return to your seat and simply watch it in silence. Over the next few minutes, the poker's glowing tip reverts from "the nature of fire" to "the nature of iron."

However many times the abbess has watched this before, she seems completely entranced. She warms up your tea and then says, "Well, it's time for evening prayer. We should be going to the chapel. Now you understand theosis. Tomorrow we could take the cold poker and put it in the sunlight. The process wouldn't be as dramatic, but you'd be surprised how much simple sunlight can overpower the nature of iron. I wonder what would happen if we put the poker right into the sun!" With that her eyes light up like a little girl's, and she shows you to the door and you return to your cottage, not overwhelmed with words, but instead, with her delight at a simple lesson in physics that for her was a lesson in spiritual formation.

After evening prayers, as you drift into sleep, you recall your conversation with the abbess. The purpose of the via purgativa is to prepare us for the via illuminativa, and the purpose of the via illuminativa is to prepare us for the via unitiva, the union of our nature with the nature of God. As we place ourselves in the light and fire of God through the practices of fotosis or illumination, we are over-powered by the nature of God, and we begin to glow with God's radiance. We join God in being fire.

One recalls Pascal's profound experience that he described in a poem that he stitched into the lining of his coat, as if to keep it close to his heart. It began:

> The year of grace 1654,
> Monday, 23 November . . .
> From about half past ten in the evening until about half past midnight, FIRE.[2]

Normal syntax can't contain what Pascal experienced during those two hours, but we get a glimpse in some of the syntactical frag-ments whose very brokenness conveys more than a complete sentence ever could: "Certitude. Certitude. Feeling. Joy. Peace. . . . Forgetfulness of the world and of everything, except GOD. . . . Greatness of the human soul. . . . Joy, joy, joy, tears of joy. . . . Jesus Christ. Jesus Christ. . . . Let me never be separated from him. . . . Renunciation, total and sweet. Complete submission to Jesus Christ."

So much about Pascal's experience is fascinating and beautiful and instructive: the fact that a brilliant mathematician would also be a mystic, the fact that an experience like this happened to some-one who articulated the famous idea of a wager—a bet on the proba-bility that God is real, the fact that Pascal never spoke or wrote of this experience, and we would know nothing of it except for this poem that was discovered in his coat after his death. But I am also intrigued by the way his poem begins, giving the date and time, more like a journalist or scientist than a poet or mystic. Why?

I think Pascal knew that this dramatic experience of Fire was extraordinary. He knew it would pass. He knew that unless he wrote something down about it, it could easily be forgotten, lost among the memories of so many other moments, one extraordinary candidate for attention that would be easily outvoted, if you will, by the millions of ordinary moments. His experience was real and mattered, but it wasn't the point, as a fascinating tension in his poem makes clear.

On the one hand, he speaks of certitude, complete submission, and renunciation. But on the other, he also speaks of separation: "I have departed from him . . . I left him; I fled him, renounced, crucified." His intense and extraordinary "baptism in fire" makes him feel as never before the horror of departing, fleeing, renouncing, and being separated from

> AS WE PLACE OURSELVES IN THE LIGHT AND FIRE OF GOD THROUGH THE PRACTICES OF FOTOSIS OR ILLUMINATION, WE ARE OVERPOWERED BY THE NATURE OF GOD, AND WE BEGIN TO GLOW WITH GOD'S RADIANCE.

the Fire and Light. And so in the midst of his sublime joy and certitude, he thinks of how the nearness can be sustained when the vision ends. He writes, "He is to be found only in the ways taught in the Gospel. . . . He is only kept securely by the ways taught in the gospel."

Notice the repetition of the word *ways*. What the mystic experiences in extraordinary moments of ecstasy—moments which by definition must be rare because otherwise they would be neither extraordinary nor ecstatic—can be found and "kept securely" through *ways*. And no doubt, the ways to which he refers are the same practices to which our abbess would refer, and in particular, the practices of theosis.

As I said earlier, the word theosis has a strange sound to my American ears. It sounds more like a disease than anything. And perhaps we could say, just as a piece of wood *catches* fire when placed with other burning logs, and just as an iron rod in some way *catches* the heat and glow of the fire in which it is plunged, and just as a person who gets too close to a person with a cold *catches* first the germs and then their symptoms from his companion, then if we are plunged into God's light and heat long enough, if we stay close enough to God for long enough, close enough to breathe God's breath, so to speak, then we will *catch* a case of God. The symptoms of what God has . . . love, joy, peace, patience, justice, purity, strength, vitality . . . will be transferred to us, and we will be infected. Theosis, in this sense, means being infected with God.

THEOSIS, IN THIS SENSE, MEANS BEING INFECTED WITH GOD.

And we could say that when we become infected, we also become carriers of the health, carriers of the healing, carriers of the vitality and light and fire, so it can spread to others and perhaps, please God, cause a full-blown pandemic.

At this point, we have come full circle, full circle in a number of ways. You may recall that earlier (in chapter 12) we asked this question: Does God's mission work from the individual to the world, or from the world to the individual? Is it a part-to-whole process or a whole-to-parts process? We may now have our answer.

Before the beginning, in the reality before what we know as reality began, God was All, and All was God. God was the Whole. Then God, in great generosity, made time and space and spoke possibility into them—"Let there be . . ."—so that other things, new things, things that had never before been, could share and experience what God alone experienced: being. Within the matrix of time and space, the possibilities unfolded and flowered in a wild creative experiment we clumsily call evolution, combining and recombining to form complex proteins and viruses, trilobites and lunged fish, stegosaurs and pterodactyls, zebras and giraffes, humpback whales and mastodons, and eventually protohominids, and finally naked apes we know as homo sapiens. We found ourselves the inheritors of amazing gifts—ultimately, gifts from God contained in the original possibility of "Let there be . . .," gifts that had appreciated like a compounding investment through millions of births and deaths, adaptations and evolutions. And tragically, we squandered our gifts, wasted our inheritance, turned our Creator's parental dreams for us and our world into the heartbreaking nightmare known too well by parents of prodigals everywhere.

We had inherited the wealth and beauty and balance created by uncountable generations of living things in a garden of possibility. We had become the CEOs of planet earth, its managers, principals, overseers. And we botched the job. We lost the plot, missed the point, forgot what it was all about. We, as Pascal said, "departed from him, left him, fled him, renounced, crucified." Tragically. Criminally. Stupidly. It was, in the truest sense of the words, a damned shame.

The result? War. Waste. Wealth at the expense of others. Stripped mountains. Eroded soil. Extinct species. Ghettoes. Genocides. Refugees, slums, squatter camps, kids begging on the sidewalks where they sleep. Slaves. Hostages. Prisoners. Obscene opulence for a few, obscene deprivation for many. Tears. Curses. Fear. Mocking laughter. Raised fists. Wailing widows, grieving mothers and fathers, orphans . . . so many orphans. Funerals. Depression. Agony. Angst. Atheism, and even worse, vicious religion.

THE CALL TO THEOSIS, THE CALL OF THE VIA UNITIVA, IS THE CALL FOR US TO REALIZE THAT WE HAVE WITHDRAWN OURSELVES FROM THE FIRE AND LOST THE GLOW OF GLORY.

The call to theosis, the call of the via unitiva, is the call for us to realize that we have withdrawn ourselves from the fire and lost the glow of glory. We have changed from what we were, and what we could again be, into something cold and hard and dead. And so some of us long for the fire. We want to rejoin God. We want to defect from the trajectory we are on, and so we begin with katharsis, and proceed through fotosis, seeking theosis. But not just for ourselves, not just for our souls. That would be only a partial healing, a pseudo-salvation, a semisalvation. To want to save my own precious soul but remain careless about the rest of humanity and the rest of creation would be to join a religion—each of which seems to care quite a bit for its own, but not so much for "the other." Joining a religion is a step in the right direction, perhaps, and no doubt some sectors of some religions would be a bigger and better step than others. But what we seek when we seek theosis goes far beyond joining a religion. We want . . . we dare . . . we refuse to settle for anything less than joining God.

We want to join God in joy. We want no happiness that God doesn't share, but we want to share God's pleasure in every little thing. We want to join God in love. We want to love what God loves—and not love what God doesn't love: pride, cruelty, fear, apathy, every bad thing. We want to join God in action, creating, reaching out, healing, empathizing, opposing, confronting, transforming, waiting, choosing, encouraging.

We want to join God in suffering, because—contrary to the Greek's understanding

WE WANT TO JOIN GOD

IN LOVE.

of the philosopher's *theos*, the God of Abraham and his descendants is a God who feels, a God who suffers. So if God is forgotten, we want to join God in being forgotten. So if God is rejected and opposed and misunderstood and misrepresented, we want to suffer each indiginity and sorrow with God. We don't enjoy suffering, but because we love God, we choose it because to stand aloof from God in God's suffering would be to reverse theosis.

We want to join God in rest and in celebration. And in the end, when our brains and hearts and bones and skin are tired, we want to join God in death just as we have joined God in life. Yes, this life has been sweet, and we have practiced—with every breath and pulse and choice—the preserving of our life. But when the time comes to join God in a kind of life that doesn't depend on hearts and lungs and hands and brains, then we let go of this life with God that is known to us so we can join God in that life that is not yet known to us. It's different—to die rather than to live—

but it's the same: to be with God, to join God, to move even deeper into the light.

That wonderful songwriter Bruce Cockburn captured this mysterious choice which is simultaneously letting go and reaching out, leaving and entering. At the death of a fellow musician, he wrote . . .

> There you go
> Swimming deeper into mystery
> Here I remain
> Only seeing where you used to be
> Stared at the ceiling
> 'Til my ears filled up with tears
> Never got to know you
>
> Suddenly you're out of here
> Gone from mystery into mystery
> Gone from daylight into night
> Another step deeper into darkness
> Closer to the light[3]

Another songwriter, Saint Francis, said something very similar:

> Be praised, my Lord, for Sister Death,
> Who will embrace all life,
> And carry us up to the arms of You.[4]

Perhaps we people of faith are the end of the fireplace poker that has entered the flame. We glow hot in the light of God, and we send heat farther and farther up the length of the iron rod. We don't seek theosis to the exclusion of other people, but for their benefit.

We seek union with God not to separate ourselves from those who are still cold and hard like iron, but to be links in a chain or a convection process that reaches from God, through us, to them. We grow hot so they can grow warm. Freely we have received, so freely we give.

Much more could be said, but it still wouldn't be enough.

SPIRITUAL EXERCISES

1. Did you perceive a change in the tone and style of the author's writing in this chapter? Why might that be?
2. Recount the parable of the fireplace poker.
3. Tell the story of creation as the story of joining God in being, separating from God in sinning, and rejoining God in abiding.
4. Ponder death as a new way of joining God.
5. Speak with God about joining God. Do so with the awareness that you are on holy ground.
6. Contrast joining God to the exclusion of others with joining God on behalf of others.

CHAPTER 19

FAITHING OUR PRACTICES

My friend Carrie Newcomer wrote a song that has touched me deeply, time and time again.

> holy is the dish and drain
> the soap and sink, and the cup and plate
> and the warm wool socks, and the cold white tile
> showerheads and good dry towels
> and frying eggs sound like psalms
> with bits of salt measured in my palm
> it's all a part of a sacrament
> as holy as a day is spent
>
> holy is the busy street
> and cars that boom with passion's beat
> and the check out girl, counting change
> and the hands that shook my hands today
> and hymns of geese fly overhead
> and spread their wings like their parents did
> blessed be the dog, that runs in her sleep

to chase some wild and elusive thing
holy is the familiar room
and quiet moments in the afternoon
and folding sheets like folding hands
to pray as only laundry can
i'm letting go of all my fear
like autumn leaves made of earth and air
for the summer came and the summer went
as holy as a day is spent

holy is the place i stand
to give whatever small good i can
and the empty page, and the open book
redemption everywhere i look
unknowingly we slow our pace
in the shade of unexpected grace
and with grateful smiles and sad lament
as holy as a day is spent

and morning light sings "providence"
as holy as a day is spent[1]

The purpose of the ancient way and the ancient practices is not to make us more religious. It is to make us more alive. Alive to God. Alive to our spouses, parents, children, neighbors, strangers, and yes, even our enemies. Alive to the house wren speeding to her nest with another caterpillar to feed her demanding brood. Alive to the cricket singing outside our back doors. Alive to the cloud that is sailing over you right now. Alive to the spin of our planet—real, but completely undetectable to us. Alive to chemistry and physics and philosophy and economics and even politics. Alive to open books and folded sheets, a sleeping dog, migrating geese, frying eggs, everything.

The end of katharsis, fotosis, and theosis is that we join God in seeing. We see a forest, but not as a speculator sees it, estimating its value in an equation that multiplies board feet by dollars, and not as a so-called developer, imagining it bulldozed and turned into a parking lot for a Burger World restaurant and Super Ninja Mouse theme park. Rather, we stand alongside God, having caught God's fire, and we join God in seeing, seeing the forest with God. Can we imagine this? We see a child born with Down syndrome or autism or HIV joining God in our seeing. We see *our* politicians and soldiers from *our* army, and we see *their* politicians and soldiers from *their* armies . . . and we see them differently when we stand with God, seeing in God's light, on fire with God as we see.

THE END OF KATHARSIS, FOTOSIS, AND THEOSIS IS THAT WE JOIN GOD IN SEEING.

And we see the normal things of our daily lives differently . . . changing a diaper, washing a dish, weeding a garden, feeding a goldfish or kitten or Great Dane, paying bills, sorting socks, mowing a lawn. When we have "caught God," when we have been united with God so that we see with God, when the nature of God has overpowered our cold and hard nature so that we catch God's glow, everything changes.

My friend Jim Henderson has a wonderful way of putting things. He knows that religious systems put on people more and more pressure: give more, read more, pray more, evangelize more, attend more, learn more, try more, work more, rest more, and fail less. It's a treadmill; it's a wonder people keep coming back for more of this kind of abuse. So, Jim says, let's stop adding more things to the divinely inspired to-do list. Instead, let's start counting what we're already doing. Or put differently, let's make the things we're already doing count.

It would be tragic for you to read this book and walk away with a longer to-do list. That's why I want us to take Jim's wisdom to heart.

My wife and I were sitting at Joyce and Peter Majendie's kitchen table in Christchurch, New Zealand, talking of faith, art, church, spiritual growth—of seeing life with God. In an offhand remark, Peter quoted a Catholic nun he had heard speak at a conference. She talked not as one might expect, of practicing our faith, but of faithing our practices. The phrase wouldn't let me go. It resonated with what Jim had been saying about counting what we're already doing.

> WHEN WE HAVE "CAUGHT GOD,"
>
> WHEN WE HAVE BEEN
>
> UNITED WITH GOD
>
> SO THAT WE SEE WITH GOD . . .
>
> EVERYTHING CHANGES.

Peter later sent me a short piece by Dr. Elizabeth Julian, RSM, the nun he had quoted. "I believe that there is a liturgy of the landscape," she wrote, "waiting to be experienced, and all are welcome at the table."[2] She invited readers to look at the practices that were meaningful to them—hiking (or "tramping" in Kiwi), walking along a beach, boating, birdwatching, exercise, sport—and to imbue these practices with meaning derived from faith.

So in recent days, I've been noticing the things I "practice"—the things I do because I enjoy them and make them habitual, the simple things that are part of daily life. I've been wondering how they can become—or how they already are—part of the ancient threefold way, practices of katharsis, fotosis, and theosis.

I take morning walks. I notice birdsongs, the progress of the seasons, changes in the weather. As I walk, of course I pray, but now I more deeply realize that my enjoyment of the season, the wind, the wildlife, the weather is a celebration of my creatureliness. It truly is an expression of my life with God. I am faithing my practice of walking.

IT WOULD BE TRAGIC FOR YOU TO READ THIS BOOK AND WALK AWAY WITH A LONGER TO-DO LIST.

I make coffee each morning. I grind beans. I smell the beans a few times, stealing a fleeting breath of their essence before and after grinding them. I boil water. I let the coffee steep a few minutes before drinking one, then two cups. Could the grinding of the beans and the releasing of their flavor become a ritual for me of katharsis, presenting my hard-bean self to God to be cracked, opened up, ground up, so the aroma of grace can flow from me? Could the reading of the morning newspaper (or Web site) become for me a ritual of fotosis, letting God's care for the world light my soul as I read of the day's crises, tragedies, and trivialities? Could that illumination flow into the union of theosis as I yield my will to join God in what God is doing internationally, nationally, locally?

I don't often enough go to the gym. But when I do, how can I faith the practice of running on the treadmill? As I inhale a needed breath, can I be expressing to God my need of grace, of strength, of sustenance—a gasp for the via illuminativa? As I exhale, can I in some way dramatize my kathartic desire to put away everything that is stale, old, dark, wrong? As I lift weights and strengthen my middle-aged muscles, can I celebrate my mobility, celebrate my age, express my desire to stay alive and flexible and vigorous with God? Can my sweat be a prayer of theosis, to join God in strength and action?

HOW CAN I FAITH THESE PRACTICES, OR DISCOVER THE KATHARSIS, FOTOSIS, AND THEOSIS ALREADY IN THEM?

As you already know, I enjoy fishing. I sneak out to a little pond near my home every chance I get. I reflect on my boyish enjoyment of luring what is hidden and elusive, hooking life and feeling its fight, and then letting it go free. What am I fishing for in life? What does the tug of the line mean to me? What intrigues me about luring out what hides in the depths outside of my sight? What joy do I get in releasing a fish after catching it? How can I faith these practices, or discover the katharsis, fotosis, and theosis already in them?

Then I move on to some less obvious practices. Dealing with traffic. Walking a few extra steps to recycle paper or plastic. Showering, getting dressed, caring for my clothing, doing yard work. What would it mean to faith each of these practices, especially the ones that get on my nerves and about which I am prone to complain?

That brings to mind the practice of keeping up with e-mail,

probably the thing I grouse about most. (I just checked with my wife. Yes, she says, it is.) Why am I always in a hurry with e-mails? What is it that I'd rather be doing than staying in touch with good people? When my in-box is full, could I experience katharsis in regard to being in a hurry to empty it? Could I let in God's light, which loves connection and fellowship and solidarity with human beings, so I see my in-box not as a pressure but as a privilege, interspersing each "send" with prayer and thanksgiving for the people I'm e-mailing? Could I join God in desiring ongoing communication and collaboration with each one? (I have a long way to go on this one.)

Looking back on my years as a pastor, I think about the kinds of people pastors care for. Moms who are barely keeping their heads above water with sick kids, work, neighborhood, church, husbands—some with no husbands, and some whose lives would be easier without the husbands they've now got.

WHAT WOULD IT MEAN TO HELP "NORMAL" PEOPLE PRACTICE THEOSIS NOT BY ADDING MORE TO THEIR SCHEDULES, BUT BY HELPING THEM REALIZE HOW MANY PEOPLE THEY ARE ALREADY JOINING GOD IN SEEING, TOUCHING, SERVING?

There are hardworking dads, widows, retirees, teenagers, unemployed folks, addicts/recovering addicts, and of course, their fellow pastors too. Then I realize that pastors are simply people who have publicly joined God in caring for others, but that really all of us are called to care for others. So we can all be undercover pastors in this way. In fact, those of us who work outside the church get to extend God's care to more people in more places than most pastors could ever imagine, just in the course of our daily lives—selling, buying, fixing, hiring, listening, teaching, collaborating, and so on. So I wonder, what would it mean to help "normal" people practice theosis, not by adding more to their schedules, but by helping them realize how many people they are already joining God in seeing, touching, serving?

THE ANCIENT WAY IS ABOUT

JOINING GOD

IN THE SPENDING OF EVERY DAY.

Then I recall a Celtic prayer I once came across, a prayer to be used each morning as one stirred the embers in the hearth: "As I stir the embers of my daily fire, I ask you, living God, to stir the embers of my heart into a flame of love for you, for my family, for my neighbor, and for my enemy." And there was another old Celtic prayer—to be said as faithful Christians splashed cold water on their faces three times in a simple morning ritual: "Let me awaken to you, Father, Son, and Holy Spirit." My new considerations turn out, as they always do, to be a rediscovery of something old and very precious.

The ancient way is about joining God in the spending of every day. When we spend our days this way, we truly save them.

SPIRITUAL EXERCISES

1. Think of your morning rituals, from showering to commuting. How might you "faith" these practices?
2. Think of your special interests and pleasures. How might you faith these practices?
3. The author seems to be aware that the book is drawing to a close. Do you feel you have gained a longer to-do list in these pages, or the opposite? How has your engagement with this book affected you so far?
4. Experiment with seeing your daily work as a way of joining God in the service of others.
5. Thank God for not needing to do more and more and more, but instead, thank God for the opportunity to gain more and more joy and meaning and purpose from what you're already doing.

CHAPTER 20

LEARNING BY (BROKEN) HEART

I think I'd like to meet Saint Francis more than any other Christian hero. I say "I think" because I'm a little worried that I would feel about him as I have felt about a few famous people whose actual presence, when I met them, was a bit of a disappointment, as I'm sure mine is to anyone who has inflated expectations of me. Saint Francis may have been a strange person in need of strong medication and pretty hard to live with. But I'd rather not know that, frankly. I'd rather think of him as a fascinating person who, as long as you don't put him on a pedestal of completely unrealistic expectations, can have a bunch of faults or eccentricities that are more or less easily ignored because of the beauty and goodness of his essential character.

Saint Francis is generally thought of as a joyful fellow, singing to birds and waltzing through fields of wildflowers with his brothers like Maria and the von Trapp children in *The Sound of Music*. In fact, his life may seem exactly like the kind of life that could be turned into a first-rate, uplifting musical. If I wanted to create such a musical, I would definitely include this story of Saint Francis reprimanding a gloomy friar with these words:

Why are you making an outward display of grief and sorrow for your sin? This sorrow is between God and yourself alone. So pray him in his mercy to pardon you and restore to your soul the joy of his salvation, of which the guilt of your sins has deprived it. Always do your best to be cheerful when you are with me and the other brethren; it is not right for a servant of God to show a sad and gloomy face, to his brother or to anyone else.

I'm quite certain that Saint Francis practiced what he preached here, which adds to his *Mary Poppins* image, adding a spoonful of sugar to every dose of bitter medicine. But if you go deeper than the typical flower-child caricature, you discover that Saint Francis, for all his simple joy, was a complex man who suffered a lot of pain. Most obvious was the fact that he chose a life of obedience, poverty, and celibacy. Any one of them would be tough, and any two, tougher, but all three together . . . enough said.

On top of that, Francis's mission drew him into close relationship with people in great pain—other poor people, lepers, criminals, other social outcasts. We could say he experienced the suffering of "the helping professions"—except that in the helping professions, you can go home at the end of the day to a well-heated, well-air-conditioned home with a hot shower and access to the History Channel and Animal Planet, while Saint Francis basically took his work home with him every night of his life. After a hard day of caring for lepers, he had a fast-growing order to lead, and many members of the order were a handful to deal with, and some of them were a downright pain in the neck or lower, lower back.

On top of this, he was deeply devoted to fasting—excessively so, he admitted in his later life. So his health wasn't the greatest, and he often suffered from severe illness. There's a fascinating story that

I don't have time to go into about how he contracted an eye infection that caused him great pain until the end of his life. All this is to say that Saint Francis may have been a joyful guy, but it isn't easy being joyful when you're a poor, celibate leader of a fast-growing order, with an ailing body and a strict vow of asceticism and your eyes itch and burn and give you stabs of pain in bright sunlight. So what Saint Francis knew about joy—to borrow again Joni Mitchell's pregnant phrase—he learned from both sides.

He was once explaining joy to a brother:

> What is perfect joy? A messenger comes and says that all the masters of Paris have entered the Order, write, "not true joy." Likewise that all the prelates beyond the Alps, archbishops and bishops; likewise that the King of France and the King of England (have entered the Order): write, "not true joy." Likewise, that my friars went among the infidels and converted them all to the faith; likewise that I have from God this grace, that I make the sick healthy and work many miracles: I say to you that in all these things there is not true joy.

In other words, he imagines all the joy that comes from success and sees through it: it is only imposter joy. He continues, creating a scene so vivid in detail that one can actually imagine it is drawn from actual experience:

> But what is true joy? I return from Perugia and in the dead of night I come here and it is winter time, muddy and what is more, so frigid, that icicles have congealed at the edge of my tunic and they always pierce my shins, and blood comes forth from such wounds. And entirely [covered] with mud and in the cold and ice, I come to the gate, and after I knock for a long time and call,

there comes a friar and he asks: "Who is it? I respond: "Friar Francis." And he says: "Go away; it is not a decent hour for going about; you will not enter." And again he would respond to my insistence: "Go away; you are a simpleton and an idiot; you do not measure up to us; we are so many and such men, that we are not in need of you!" And I stand again at the gate and I say: "For the love of God take me in this night." And he would respond: "I will not." I say to you that if I will have had patience and will not have been upset, that in this is true joy and true virtue and soundness of soul.

Some people are naturally happy, born with the blessing of a cheerful demeanor the way other people are born with beautiful hair, an ugly nose, a predisposition to baldness, or a big backside. Those sunshiny people, though, are often the ones to go most ballistic when things get below a certain point of acceptability. Francis's story goes about four basements below the ground floor of anyone's acceptability level. To achieve that kind of true joy, one needs more than the common grace of a good personality. One needs the "soundness of soul" that comes through following a sound way of spiritual practice for many years, through "many dangers, toils, and snares," as the old hymn says.

This is why the ancient practices often involve memorization and recitation, which many people associate with the dreaded words *by rote*. There are times, the ancient way teaches us, when life is so unimaginably hard that stodgy old practices like memorization and recitation can practically save your life, or your sanity.

I've had a few of those times in my life. One was in my twenties, right after I had done something about which I was terribly ashamed. The cliché "racked with guilt" took on meaning for me that day. I know for some people that sounds rather old-fashioned and psychologically unhealthy, but I agree with the great sages Garrison Keillor (from his monologue "Smokes") and Danny Devito (from his movie *The Big Kahuna*) that guilt and regret, for all their inconvenience and potential for neuroses, are essential equipment in the development of a good life, and as much as we hate them, we'd be in deep trouble without them.

But we can be pretty miserable with them too, and I was. I had just done one of the shabbiest and stupidest things I had yet done in my young life, although I've broken that record several times since. It involved . . . well, I don't need to go into that. Anyway, I felt terrible. I had crossed the line, I was certain, of what was forgivable by God. Any self-respecting Supreme Being would send me to the showers, drop me from the team, cancel my membership card, and change the locks on my office door. I felt hopeless. I believed in God, in Jesus, in the Holy Spirit, in salvation by grace through faith alone. I may even have still held Calvinist opinions at that point, believing myself to be one of the elect few. But no matter. I felt a howling tornado of condemnation roaring around my soul, which was about to

> THERE ARE TIMES,
>
> THE ANCIENT WAY TEACHES US,
>
> WHEN LIFE IS SO UNIMAGINABLY
>
> HARD THAT STODGY OLD
>
> PRACTICES LIKE MEMORIZATION
>
> AND RECITATION CAN
>
> PRACTICALLY SAVE YOUR LIFE,
>
> OR YOUR SANITY.

implode. If God was trying to say, "Neither do I condemn you. Go and sin no more," or anything like that, I couldn't have heard it for the roaring.

My conscience had a raging fever, eliciting horrible hallucinations of lifelong regret or eternal damnation or one followed by the other. The possibility of forgiveness and recovery seemed nil. I couldn't think straight, and certainly couldn't pray beyond, "Oh God," because where a prayer would have followed, I would lapse into whipping myself. "Oh God . . . I'm really stupid. Oh God . . . I really blew it this time. Oh God . . . what was I thinking?" By that point "Oh God" was working less as an invocation and more as a breaking of the "taking the Lord's name in vain" commandment.

I was driving a car at this point, dangerously under the influence of guilt, and in desperation, I recited the Lord's Prayer, which I had learned but hardly ever actually used, being from a rigidly nonliturgical tradition. Once, twice, three times I said it. I thought of the passage in the Sermon on the Mount that said we should never pray with "vain repetition," but I was desperate, so I kept repeating the prayer, even if doing so was a sin. And it wasn't. It was a godsend. It put sane words into my mind and heart, words that created one still point in the midst of my temporary guilt-induced insanity, and gradually that still point spread grace, and I survived.

I had another of those shaky times the other night. I got what is probably the second worst news of my life, but may actually be the worst, because the earlier worst news I got actually turned around and came out okay, and this news feels like it can't possibly turn out okay, and that's all that needs to be said. I was also far from home, alone, jet-lagged, and in a hotel room, any one of which can make even moderately bad news seem a lot worse than it is, and this bad news didn't need any help to seem absolutely bad. I don't know exactly how to describe what I felt. The only word that comes to mind is *brokenhearted*. And *helpless*. And *in pain*. None of these words gives me any satisfaction of actually describing what I felt. I might add that if my pain had a color, it was a horrible grey that sucked the color out of everything else, and if my helplessness had a color, it was a blinding white that terrified me, because I thought I might go blind, and if my brokenheartedness had a color, it was a dark, clotted, disgusting red, for obvious reasons. And I was in the middle of that for all of the long hours of a long night, and there was nothing I could about it.

Like that day in my twenties, driving under the influence of guilt, I couldn't even pray, in the sense of forming a prayer of my own thoughts. The closest thing to a prayer that I could muster was, "So much pain. So much pain." It felt less like a prayer to God and more a report to the universe. Anyway, it was bad, and there was nowhere to go and nothing to do but, in a sense, to lie on my hotel bed and spread out my arms and legs on this cross of bad news and suffer until the suffering was done washing over me, which it still isn't, by the way. But sometime in my suffering, a memorized prayer managed to fight its way from my memory into my consciousness and started saying itself. It's known as the Jesus Prayer, and there are a few versions of it, but my version is, "Lord Jesus Christ, Son of the living God, have mercy on me a sinner." I learned this prayer maybe twenty years ago, I think from a book by a Greek Orthodox priest, which I long ago gave away and so can't check to be sure. I decided to try it, to memorize it and repeat it and see what happens.

Again, I did this against my religious upbringing, which as I said didn't believe in memorizing and reciting prayers, but required all prayers to be "from the heart," meaning spontaneous. But I'm glad I violated my upbringing because I discovered that learning something *by* heart can save you when your heart is broken so nothing can come *from* it except tears, and spontaneity is simply another burden on an already overburdened soul.

I am experiencing this memorized prayer even now, days later. It feels like an engine running in my mind, as if the power went out and this prayer is the generator that's keeping me going.

I read recently about some members of the Christian Peacemaker Teams who were kidnapped and held as hostages in Iraq for 118 days. They remarked how the things they memorized had sustained them in their days of terror and boredom.

When the pilot of your plane dies of a heart attack, it's too late for you to go into the cockpit and figure out how to fly. When the biopsy comes back *positive* (which is *negative*), it's too late to learn how to have peace in the face of death. When the towers fall and you're in them, or your significant other is in them, it's too late to learn how to have strength in adversity. When your child tells you she's gay, or your spouse tells you there's someone at work, or your best friend tells you that your drinking has been way over the line for the last few years and everyone knows it but you, it's too late to draw on reserves of strength and courage and love that you've never created.

> **LEARNING SOMETHING *BY* HEART CAN SAVE YOU WHEN YOUR HEART IS BROKEN SO NOTHING CAN COME *FROM* IT EXCEPT TEARS, AND SPONTANEITY IS SIMPLY ANOTHER BURDEN ON AN ALREADY OVERBURDENED SOUL.**

The ancient way is about building up those reserves when they're not needed so they're available when they are. It's about practicing things by heart so they'll be accessible when your heart is broken. It's about practicing landing a plane in a thunderstorm on the flight simulator so that when the storm is raging and you're low on fuel, you don't panic and crash.

Back to Saint Francis: once he stood before the sultan of Egypt. This would be, today, like a Southern Baptist getting a private audience with Osama bin Laden. Francis stood before this man who was hated by his nation and his religion, and Francis radiated love for him. He stood before this man who could have him killed like a bug, but with a thousand times more torture than any bug is capable of, and Francis radiated courage and peace. He stood before this man who represented the forces of Islam that were in a medieval death-match with the forces of Christianity, battling (among other things) over control of the ancient Jewish city of Jerusalem, which—insert ironic emoticons here—means "city of shalom" or "city of peace." And Francis radiated not a spirit of conquest and war, or a spirit of cowardice and appeasement, but rather a courageous spirit of reconciliation and love. And this in spite of the fact that his infected eyes were probably burning and itching and stabbing him with pain.

But with a deeper kind of insight, Saint Francis saw a possibility: that Islam (passionate and alive in the sultan) and Christianity (aglow within his own heart) could stop fighting over the ancient city of Judaism (Jerusalem), and instead, the three religions could dream a dream of peace together. For Francis, a believer in Jesus as the Prince of Peace, this dream came naturally, and he dared to take a stand.

Saint Francis's experiences of suffering in the years leading up to that day had become for him a crucible. The spiritual practices to which he was devoted had become for him a way of purgation, illumination, and union with God. Because he had been trained through the practices of katharsis, fotosis, and theosis in the crucible of suffering, he joined God in facing the sultan, glowing like an ember of holiness and peace. Neither side was ready to reconcile, and so the war went on. But Saint Francis is in a sense still standing there, still holding the dream, as a kind of icon, inviting us to seize the unimagined opportunities offered us by the ancient way and the ancient practices, for today and for tomorrow too, which holds dangers and possibilities we cannot imagine.[1]

Jews, Christians, and Muslims share this ancient way and these ancient practices. The ancient way is the way we must learn by heart, and we will learn it best by hearts that have been softened, if not broken, by suffering. Our choice, it seems, is whether we will let our past and present sufferings be sufficient to soften and break us, or whether we will resist and harden ourselves so even more suffering is required.

> **THE ANCIENT WAY IS THE WAY WE MUST LEARN BY HEART, AND WE WILL LEARN IT BEST BY HEARTS THAT HAVE BEEN SOFTENED, IF NOT BROKEN, BY SUFFERING.**

Our religions—all three of them—have at least in some respects lost their way. If we are not too proud to admit this most obvious but most inconvenient and painful truth, we can find our way again. Perhaps it is in letting go of the pretensions of our religions that we will begin to reduce the tensions between them. And perhaps it is in rediscovering the ancient way—that waits like a seed to germinate within each one—we will find a way to live in peace, within and among our religions. Perhaps in that way, instead of tearing the fabric of community with religiously vicious language and instead of destroying our world through religiously inspired violence, we can work together to heal it—each in our own way—with saving love.

I began this book with three reasons to pursue the ancient way of spiritual practices. First, I said, spiritual practices help develop *character*, the kind of character we see in Saint Francis standing as a man of peace before the sultan. Second, they help us be *awake* and alive and more fully human, as this singer of songs, lover of birds, embracer of lepers, and carrier of joy so clearly was. Third, they help us *experience God*, or as we have said more recently, they help us join God so that we glow with Francis like holy embers radiant with the fire of God.

And I said there was a fourth reason, which I hope is now clear, even if I haven't yet made it explicit.

If we do not rediscover in our three religions the ancient way of spiritual practice, which is perhaps the best and truest thing about them, then we will contribute to the destruction of the world. But what can happen if we find our way again, if we defect from our current highway of crusade and jihad, of intifada and apartheid, of holocaust and so-called holy war, and instead we stand with Saint Francis and fulfill that dream of his that is alive, even though he died?

That is the fourth great reason to pursue the ancient way in which we learn to practice peace, joy, self-mastery, and justice: because the future of the world depends on people like you and me finding it and living it and inviting others to join us. Maybe John Lennon was really close to being right in the old song "Imagine." Maybe "the world will be as one," not when we imagine there's no heaven as he suggested, but instead when the harmony of heaven (Jesus called it "kingdom"—but I think "harmony" is a pretty good synonym) comes to earth.[1] And maybe imagining that happening is a lot like having faith; in fact, maybe that song was John Lennon's way of saying, beautifully even if imprecisely, "May your kingdom come, may your will be done on earth as it is in heaven." And maybe the ancient way is about letting that harmony spread in and through our lives.

THAT IS THE FOURTH GREAT REASON TO PURSUE THE ANCIENT WAY . . . BECAUSE THE FUTURE OF THE WORLD DEPENDS ON PEOPLE LIKE YOU AND ME FINDING IT AND LIVING IT AND INVITING OTHERS TO JOIN US.

What if there is a treasure hidden in the field of our three great monotheisms, long buried but waiting to be rediscovered? And what if that treasure is a way . . . a way that can train us to stop killing and hating and instead to work together, under God, joining God, to build a better world, a city of peace, a city of God? What if our suffering and fear are not intended to inspire deadly cycles of defense and counterattack in a vain search for peace through victory and domination, but instead, what if they can serve to break and soften us like a plowed field after rain so that the seed of God's kingdom—a few notes of God's eternal harmony—can grow within us and among us?

This is my hope. And this is our hope. Amen.

SPIRITUAL EXERCISES

1. Reread the quotes from Saint Francis in this chapter. What do they say to you today?
2. Reflect on the phrase *learn by heart*. How does "by heart" differ from "by rote"? How can one change into the other?
3. Reflect on the fourth reason for rediscovering the ancient practices. Do you believe the author overstates the potential power of these practices? Why or why not?
4. If you know John Lennon's song "Imagine," putting its atheism aside, how would you see it as an expression of desire for what Jesus called "the kingdom of God"?
5. Imagine the scene of Saint Francis standing before the sultan. Imagine yourself standing beside him, standing with him. What would you say to Saint Francis? To the sultan? To God?
6. On a map, find Jerusalem, or find a picture of it online or in a book or magazine. Feel the irony of its name: City of Peace. Pray for the three great monotheistic religions: Judaism, Christianity, and Islam. Pray for peace. Pray that a resurgence of authentic spiritual practices will bend each toward the way of God's peace.
7. Leaf back through this book. Notice any marginal jottings or underlinings you've made. Take a few minutes in silence. Then pray whatever comes to mind and heart. You might want to pray standing, with your hands out, palms up, as an act of solidarity with your cousins in the Abrahamic tradition, expressing to God that you are waiting in receptivity and hope with open hands, that your hands hold no weapon, and that in your heart you want to be made, with Saint Francis, an instrument of peace.

STUDY GUIDE

Finding Our Way Again: The Return of the Ancient Practices

BRIAN MCLAREN

"Stand at the crossroads and look; ask for the ancient paths, ask where the good way is, and walk in it, and you will find rest for your souls."
JEREMIAH 6:16

FOREWORD, CHAPTER 1

What do you think it means to live as a "culturally safe Christian?" Are there times in your life when you've chosen "safe" over an observant and authentic faith?

PART 1: WAY

CHAPTER 1: SEARCHING FOR AN EVERYDAY SACREDNESS

Have you ever considered incorporating practices from other traditions (chanting, repetitive prayers, meditation, etc.) into your everyday life? Do you think such practices would add or detract from your faith?

In what ways do you practice your faith as a way of life as well as a system of beliefs? In what ways does "living your faith" strengthen it?

CHAPTER 2: WHY SPIRITUAL PRACTICES MATTER

In what ways does the character you want to have differ from the character you've actually been developing?

What spiritual practices do you think could aid you toward developing the depth of character you desire?

In what ways do you think these spiritual practices could make you feel more alive, more human, more humane?

How do you think being "alive to God" would change your relationships with your friends, colleagues, and family?

CHAPTER 3: THE GENESIS OF PRACTICE

Why do you think faith has more resonance when it's a part of a spiritual journey?

How does being "satisfied" with where we are in our relationship with God keep us from growing closer to Him and each other?

How does the regularity of spiritual practices provide both stability in your faith and push you toward the unknown in your spiritual journey?

CHAPTER 4: PRACTICING THE WAY OF JESUS

Have you or someone you care about experienced pain from the doctrines or dogma of the church?

What questions would you ask of someone who's avoided religion because of established doctrines?

What advantages or disadvantages might go along with a decision to follow the way of Christ without being a part of an established church?

CHAPTER 5: PAUL AND THE WAY OF LOVE

How do you think your daily life would change if you practiced your faith as an expression of love between you and those around you? How would this change the way you interact with people at the office? In traffic? At the grocery store?

Why do you think Paul compared the practice of faith in Jesus to physical exercise? What benefits do a "faith expressing itself through love" and running a race have in common?

CHAPTER 6: SHARING TREASURES AMONG FRIENDS

In what ways do you find that your spiritual experiences have become "formulaic"?

In what ways have you sought to grow your faith in the past? Are there elements of what you've done before that still help you grow, or have they stopped working?

What value do you think the practices of other "cooking schools" hold for you?

CHAPTER 7: OPEN-SOURCE SPIRITUALITY

In what ways have your own spiritual mentors forced your faith to stretch and grow? How would you like to pass on what they taught you to others?

Who surprised you the most by sharing something about their own faith? Why were you surprised?

CHAPTER 8: SHALLOW TROUBLE, DEEP TROUBLE

During the times you have felt lost or distracted from your faith journey, were you drifting from the path or the destination? How did you try to regain your focus?

In what ways is your faith already balanced between the "Activist Way" and the "Contemplative Way"? How do these two approaches to faith blend in your life?

PART 2: PRACTICES

CHAPTER 9: PRACTICE MAKES POSSIBLE

Have you ever been a part of a community or group that helped you achieve an "impossible" goal (weight loss, spiritual discipline, physical fitness, overcoming addiction, etc.)? In what ways did the community provide the tools to achieve what you could not alone?

Skaters often find that their skating is stronger from practicing the basics. In the same way, even professional musicians practice the basics. Have you ever given up on training of any kind because of the tedium of practice? How could a community keep you focused on a long-term goal?

CHAPTER 10: CONTEMPLATIVE PRACTICES

How do you feel about the idea that contemplative times with God can lead to "the experience of living God in this life"?

Have you ever fallen into the belief that if you "pray right," then God always answers prayers? How can such a belief lead into unreasonable expectations of how God works in our lives?

CHAPTER 11: COMMUNAL PRACTICES

When you attend communal services, what steps do you take to prepare yourself for the worship and truly engage your mind in the words of the liturgy?

What advantages do you take for your communal worship—the inward journey into *we*—that aid and support your private practices—that inward journey into *me*?

CHAPTER 12: MISSIONAL PRACTICES

If our missonal practices were more fully integrated into the world around us, what changes could you foresee taking place in your own church? Your own community?

If you put five (or more) of the practices of the via active to work, what changes do you think would happen in your own life?

CHAPTER 13: THE CYCLE WE FIND OURSELVES IN

How can a church or religious group avoid falling into an "us vs. them" mentality, which can be a step toward spiritual blindness?

What internal checks can a group make on itself to ensure that their goals are still biblically sound? How can we make sure we haven't "propped our ladder against the wrong building"?

CHAPTER 14: MOVING ON

Has your comfort with tradition or your current beliefs led you to reject new ideas without investigating their validity?

When you see God working strongly with another church, are you curious about their beliefs? Do you ever wish you could bring a little of what is happening to other believers into your own life or church? What's stopping you?

Why do you think we as believers tend to reject anything new, even if we see God's hand in the work?

PART 3: ANCIENT

CHAPTER 15: PRACTICING THE ANCIENT WAY

In what ways does your current community encourage your faith be active, even "breathless"? Is this the kind of faith you desire?

In what ways do you think that following ancient practices, such as constant prayer or fasting, could lead you to an vital, active faith?

CHAPTER 16: KATHARSIS (VIA PURGATIVA)

Are there areas in your life where the three main "black holes"— pride, lust, greed—could take hold and lead your heart and mind astray? What part does fear play in making these three attractive?

In what ways could a "vulnerability group" help you right now?

CHAPTER 17: FOTOSIS (VIA ILLUMINATIVA)

C.S. Lewis once wrote: "I believe in Christianity as I believe that the sun has risen: not only because I see it, but because by it I see everything else." In what ways does this quote reflect the fotosis, as described in this chapter?

Have there been times when you felt God drawing you closer to Him, in the way the sun draws flowers to turn to the light? Have you resisted?

How do you think viewing your world in the light of God could help you cope with the everyday trials and busyness of our world?

CHAPTER 18: THEOSIS (VIA UNITIVA)

How do you think the purging of our darkness and the embracing of God's light prepare us to unite with Him, to feel and share the fire He can give all believers?

Have you ever craved that "fire" of God in your life? How do you think it would transform you? Can you see yourself reflecting it, sharing it with those you love?

CHAPTER 19: FAITHING OUR PRACTICES

When you care for others, how is this a reflection of God's light in your life? When you look at the people you love and care about, can you see the ways God uses them in your life?

Is there one regular activity, more than the others, which could be used to remind you of God's presence in your life?

CHAPTER 20: LEARNING BY (BROKEN) HEART

What have you learned during your faith journey that can sustain you when your worst trials hit, when your heart is fully broken?

Given the chance to stand before your worst enemy, what would you say to him or her? Would you be able to radiate God's love or would you want to pour out your grievances?

Why do you think it is the trials in our lives, our broken hearts, that give us a stronger faith, a stronger unity with God? How do we use that unity to grow spiritually and to reach out to others?

NOTES

ACKNOWLEDGMENTS

1. See especially Richard J. Foster, *Celebration of Discipline: The Path to Spiritual Growth* (San Francisco: HarperOne, 2002); Dallas Willard, *The Divine Conspiracy: Rediscovering Our Hidden Life in God* (San Francisco: HarperOne, 1998); Eugene Peterson, *Christ Plays in Ten Thousand Places: A Conversation in Spiritual Theology* (Grand Rapids: Wm. B. Eerdmans Publishing Co., 2005), and Joan Chittister, *Wisdom Distilled from the Daily: Living the Rule of St. Benedict Today* (San Francisco: HarperOne, 1991).

2. See especially Jim Wallis, *Faith Works: Lessons from the Life of an Activist Preacher* (New York: Random House, 2000) and *The Great Awakening: Reviving Faith and Politics in a Post-Religious Right America* (San Francisco: HarperOne 2008); Tony Campolo and Mary Darling, *The God of Intimacy and Action: Reconnecting Ancient Spiritual Practices, Evangelism, and Justice* (San Francisco: Jossey-Bass, 2007); and Ron Sider, *Rich Christians in an Age of Hunger: Moving from Affluence to Generosity* (Nashville: Thomas Nelson, 2005).

3. Tony's book *The Sacred Way: Spiritual Practices for Everyday Life* (Grand Rapids: Zondervan, 2005) remains my favorite short introduction to spiritual practices; it's an underrated treasure. Doug's *Reimagining Spiritual Formation: A Week in the Life of an Experimental Church* (Grand Rapids: Zondervan, 2004) and Doug Pagitt and Kathryn Prill, *Body Prayer: The Posture of Intimacy with God* (Colorado Springs: WaterBrook, 2005), along with Diana's *Christianity for the Rest of Us: How the Neighborhood Church is Transforming the Faith* (San Francisco: HarperOne, 2007) and *The Practicing Congregation: Imagining a New Old Church* (Herndon, VA: Alban, 2004) are also wonderful resources from important leaders in the recovery of Christian faith as way. Also among the growing treasury of helpful books on spiritual practices, I would highlight Ruth Haley Barton, *Invitation to Silence and Solitude: Experiencing God's Transforming Presence* (Downer's Grove, IL: InterVarsity Press, 2004); Scott McKnight, *Praying with the Church: Developing a Daily Rhythm for Spiritual Formation* (Brewster, MA: Paraclete, 2006); Joni Grace Powers and Robert Pyne, *LifeSpace: The Practice of Life with God* (Ventura, CA: Regal, 2007); and Daniel Wolpert, *Creating a Life with God: The Call of Ancient Prayer Practices* (Nashville: Upper Room Books, 2003).

CHAPTER 3: THE GENESIS OF PRACTICE

1. For our purposes in this book, we will take the sacred narratives at face value. We won't try to force them into modern categories such as "literal, historical, scientific fact" or "primitive myth." We will simply assume that, because they are part of the sacred texts shared by the three Abrahamic faiths, they are formative and authoritative in each faith community, whether or not they are in every detail absolutely historical in the modern sense.

2. We could also say that sacrifices were also a kind of sacred meal, as the things typically sacrificed—some grain, a goat, a lamb, a bull—were the makings of a meal. In fact, in Leviticus 6:26, 29, they're identified in exactly this way.

3. Perhaps this exchange represents Abraham discovering a soul mate, an authentic spiritual kinship with "the other."

4. I should add that fasting reminds the community at large of hunger—the common experience of the poor—and Sabbath gives the poor the same day off that the rich enjoy. More could be said about the ways in which the ancient practices relink the poor with their neighbors, evoking the etymology of religion.

CHAPTER 4: PRACTICING THE WAY OF JESUS

1. See, for example, Brian McLaren, *The Secret Message of Jesus: Uncovering the Truth That Could Change Everything* (Nashville: Thomas Nelson, 2007).

2. Sadly, Jesus' statement "I am the way, and the truth, and the life. No one comes to the Father except through me" (John 14:6) is one of the most frequently misunderstood statements in the Bible. I have written about it elsewhere—including in an article entitled "A Reading of John 14:6," available at my Website: http://www.brianmclaren.net/emc/archives/McLaren%20-%20John%2014.6.pdf.

3. The apostle Paul uses this language in 2 Timothy 2:2, 1 Corinthians 11:1, and elsewhere.

4. Latin American theologian Harold Segura emphasizes the following of Jesus in this way: "Christian spirituality is not only having faith in Jesus but also having the faith of Jesus." ("Jesus in the Face of the Needy," *Journal of Latin American Theology* (February 2006), 114.

CHAPTER 5: PAUL AND THE WAY OF LOVE

1. I was actually taught the opposite of this approach, namely that the meat of Paul's writings was to be found at the beginning, with a kind of postscript of practical application at the end. Agreement with the first-half concepts was required and central; following the second-half way was elective follow-up. I'm suggesting that the two halves cannot be separated so easily; the first-half what of "theory" prepares for the second half so-what of "practice," and the second-half "way" assumes the first-half "why."

2. I once described the difference between learning about and learning in an article in *Leadership* journal:

> When I taught people to play guitar, I wasn't just teaching them about the guitar—how many strings there are, what frets do, or why the grain of the soundboard is important. True, I would be interested in sharing this information; it would be of some value. But I was interested in teaching guitar. When I was a writing teacher, it was the same: it wasn't just information I was interested in transferring. I was actually interested in helping my students become the kind of people who could think clearly and feel honestly and convey those thoughts and feelings in words, phrases, sentences, and paragraphs. It was the same with literature. Yes, there was an "about" dimension, but it was always in service of the direct, transforming, empowering encounter—learning interpretation, learning literature, learning poetry, beyond about.

> Brian McLaren, "Informed, but Not Transformed: Too Many 'Educated' Christians Have Gotten Lots of Information but Are the Least Christ-like," *Leadership* journal, August 15, 2005. Available at http://jmm.aaa.net.au/articles/15655.htm.

3. Thanks to Dallas Willard for this important idea.

4. This bearing of Christ in the world is captured in Gerard Manley Hopkins's beautiful line, "Christ plays in ten thousand places," from "As Kingfishers Catch Fire," 1918 (public domain), available at http://www.bartleby.com/122/34.html.

CHAPTER 6: SHARING TREASURES AMONG FRIENDS

1. Jay Olson, "A Return to Tradition: A New Interest in Old Ways takes Root in Catholicism and Many Other Faiths," *U. S. News and World Report*, December 13, 2007, http://www.usnews.com:80/articles/news/national/2007/12/13/a-return-to-traditional.html.

CHAPTER 7: OPEN SOURCE SPIRITUALITY

1. Some believe progress in this area has been hindered by Pope John Paul II's Christifideles Laici in 1988, and coincidentally furthered by the practical shortage of priests.

CHAPTER 8: SHALLOW TROUBLE, DEEP TROUBLE

1. On atheism, see Becky Garrison, *The New Atheist Crusaders and Their Unholy Grail* (Nashville: Thomas Nelson, 2008). Also see her *Rising from the Ashes* (New York: Seabury, 2007).

2. See, for example, Brian McLaren, *The Last Word and the Word After That: A Tale of Faith, Doubt, and a New Kind of Christianity* (New York: Jossey-Bass, 2005).

3. Some astute readers are no doubt asking, "Can't we have the best of both options?" In other words, could we lean our ladder against a building called "Seeking God's Kingdom on Earth, and Anticipating an Afterlife with God?" This is, I would agree, the ideal option and the one I myself try to live by, but I have stopped short of it in this chapter in order to press other ideas home more strongly.

4. When I addressed this subject in my previous book, *Everything Must Change: Jesus, Global Crises, and a Revolution of Hope* (Nashville: Thomas Nelson, 2007), I was intrigued by two common responses. Some people said, "McLaren is creating a straw man. Hardly anybody actually promotes that kind of unidimensional gospel of evacuation. We who focus on hell-avoidance and the afterlife are also very involved in good works and in addressing the social problems of this life." But others—in surprising numbers and with surprising vehemence—said the opposite: "McLaren is a liberal and a heretic. The only true gospel is about the destiny of the soul after this life. The true gospel has nothing to say about social concerns." A surprising number of bloggers reaffirmed their rather flattened understanding of the gospel, arguing at length with aspects of the book's theology while completely ignoring what it said about poverty, war, and the environment. Equally surprising, one notable American Christian author and preacher asserted, in a radio interview widely distributed on the Internet, that Jesus had no social agenda and that he had no interest in ending poverty or slavery. Jesus didn't come, this respected preacher said, "to fix something in somebody's life for the little moment that they live on this earth." Jesus came for one reason and one reason only, he affirmed: "to seek and save the lost"—which, in his estimation, does not include being saved from slavery or poverty "in this little moment they live on earth." "Seeking and saving the lost" only means saving the soul from hell after death. So, although I have no desire to create a straw man, I am interested in pointing out how the gospel of evacuation remains powerful, influential, vigorous, and more prevalent than many people realize. As I said in *Everything Must Change*, these two very different understandings of what "save" means lead to very

different understandings of what it means to be a follower of the Savior and a practitioner of his way. (www.youtube. com/watch?v=OH1Omij7Q4)

5. Later, we'll add a third element by supplementing contemplative and activist practices with social, communal, or public practices.

6. See Tony Campolo and Mary Darling, *The God of Intimacy and Action: Reconnecting Ancient Spiritual Practices, Evangelism, and Justice* (San Francisco: Jossey-Bass, 2007).

CHAPTER 9: PRACTICE MAKES POSSIBLE

1. See Chapter 13.

CHAPTER 10: CONTEMPLATIVE PRACTICES

1. Thanks to Dallas Willard for this distinction between effort and earning.

CHAPTER 11: COMMUNAL PRACTICES

1. Based on Joni Mitchell, "Both Sides Now," ©1967 Crazy Crow Music/ Sony/ATV Tunes LLC. ASCAP.

2. Doug Pagitt offers a creative response to both the hermeneutic of suspicion and its opposite, the precritical or naive hermeneutic. In *Preaching Re-Imagined* (Grand Rapids: Zondervan, 2005), he encourages churches to complement sermons with dialogue, where the congregation interacts with the preacher, posing questions, sharing experiences, challenging questionable points, offering counterpoints. This dialogical "preaching without speeching" creates a sense of heightened mutuality between preacher and congregation. It allows the congregation to test the speaker, constructively engaging suspicious listeners, and it invites and even challenges naive listeners to think for themselves and have a voice, not merely be passive receivers of the preacher's speechings."

3. See Mike Mason, *Practicing the Presence of People: How We Learn to Love* (Colorado Springs: Waterbrook, 1999).

CHAPTER 12: MISSIONAL PRACTICES

1. For more on Jim Wallis's work, go to sojo.net, and read *God's Politics* (HarperSanFrancisco, 2006) and *The Great Awakening* (HarperSanFrancisco, 2008).

CHAPTER 13: THE CYCLE WE FIND OURSELVES IN

1. Michael Polanyi, *Personal Knowledge: Towards a Post: Critical Philosophy* (Oxford: Routledge, 1958, rev. ed. 1997), 53.
2. See David Kinnaman and Gabe Lyons, *Unchristian:* What a New Generation Really Thinks About Christianity . . . *and Why it Matters* (Grand Rapids; Baker, 2007) and Alan Jamieson, *A Churchless Faith* (Pilgrim Press, 2002).

CHAPTER 14: MOVING ON

1. Jewish and Muslim readers could imagine a similar kind of diagram with quadrants or zones of their own, such as Sunni, Shiite, and Sufi, or Reconstructionist, Reformed, Orthodox, and Conservative.

CHAPTER 15: PRACTICING THE ANCIENT WAY

1. See *Finding Faith: A Search for What Makes Sense* (Grand Rapids: Zondervan, 2007), esp. the chapter entitled, "How Does Faith Grow?"
2. For a wonderful introduction to the three-fold way of katharsis, fotosis, and theosis, written by a sociologist rather than a religious professional, see Kyriacos C. Markides, *The Mountain of Silence: A Search for Orthodox Spirituality* (New York: Image, 2001).

CHAPTER 17: FOTOSIS

1. *The Weight of Glory* by C.S. Lewis copyright © 1965 C.S. Lewis Pte. Ltd.

CHAPTER 18: THEOSIS

1. As an evangelical Protestant, I was taught to use different language to point toward the same experience. For us, purgation/katharsis was described in terms of justification, being saved or born again. We focused on the fact that our sins were forgiven and we were saved from condemnation and hell. We were careful to confess our sins, believing (based on 1 John 1:9) that God would be "faithful and just to forgive us our sins." Illumination/fotosis was, for us, contained in the word *sanctification*, the process of becoming more holy. We spoke of "spiritual growth" and "discipleship" and "Christian education" to approximate the idea of gradual fotosis. Because of our emphasis on total depravity and the radical effects of original sin, most of us shied away from the idea of union/theosis; that would occur after this life when, recalling 1 John 3:1, we would see Christ and then be like him. However, many of us leaned toward the idea of theosis with terms such as "entire sanctification" or "the deeper life" or "the exchanged life" or "total commitment" and "total surrender" and "wholehearted devotion," and those of us who were Pentecostal or charismatic touched on it through the idea of being filled with the Holy Spirit.

2. For these and other quotes from Blaise Pascal in this chapter, see Brian McLaren, *A Generous Orthodoxy* (Grand Rapids: Zondervan, 2004), 164–65.

3. Bruce Cockburn, "Changed by the Light," © 1994 BMI. All rights reserved. Used with permission.

4. This is from my rendering of Saint Francis's "Canticle of the

Sun." It is available for purchase on CD or download at
www.restorationvillage.com.

CHAPTER 19: FAITHING OUR PRACTICES

1. Carrie Newcomer, "Holy As a Day Is Spent"
2. Brian McLaren, "Practicing Faith, or Faithing our Practices?"
   Christianity Today, 22 June 2006.

CHAPTER 20 LEARNING BY (BROKEN) HEART

1. For an important book on Muslim–Christian dialogue, see Mark
   Siljander, *A Deadly Misunderstanding* (San Francisco: HarperOne,
   2008).
1. John Lennon, "Imagine," © 1971 Lenono Music/ BMI.

ABOUT THE AUTHOR

Brian D. McLaren is an author, speaker, pastor, and networker among innovative Christian leaders, thinkers, and activists.

Born in 1956, McLaren graduated from University of Maryland with degrees in English (BA, summa cum laude, 1978, and MA, in 1981). He was awarded a Doctor of Divinity Degree (honoris causa) in 2004 from Carey Theological Seminary. From 1978 to 1986, McLaren taught college English, and in 1982, he helped form Cedar Ridge Community Church, an innovative, nondenominational church in the Baltimore-Washington area (crcc.org). He left higher education in 1986 to serve as the church's founding pastor and served in that capacity until 2006.

McLaren is a popular conference speaker and a frequent guest lecturer at seminaries and denominational gatherings, nationally and internationally. He has also appeared on *Larry King Live*, *Religion and Ethics Newsweekly*, and *Nightline*. His work has also been covered in Time (where he was listed as one of American's 25 most influential evangelicals), *Christianity Today*, *Christian Century*, the *Washington Post*, and many other print media.

His books include *A Generous Orthodoxy* (Emergent/YS/Zondervan, 2004), *The Secret Message of Jesus* (Thomas Nelson, 2006), and *Everything Must Change* (Thomas Nelson, 2007). His books have been or are being translated into many languages, including Korean, Chinese, French, Swedish, Norwegian, German, and Spanish.

He serves as a board chair for Sojourners (sojo.net), and is a founding member of Red Letter Christians, a group of communicators seeking to broaden and deepen the dialogue about faith and public life.

Brian is married to Grace, and they have four young adult children. More information can be found at his websites, brianmclaren.net and deepshift.org.

THE ANCIENT PRACTICES SERIES

PHYLLIS TICKLE, GENERAL EDITOR

Finding Our Way Again by Brian McLaren

In Constant Prayer by Robert Benson

Sabbath by Dan B. Allender

Fasting by Scot McKnight

Tithing by Douglas LeBlanc

The Sacred Meal by Nora Gallagher

The Liturgical Year by Joan Chittister

The Sacred Journey by Charles Foster

*Stand at the crossroads and look; ask for the ancient paths,
ask where the good way is, and walk in it,
and you will find rest for your souls.*

—JEREMIAH 6:16 NIV

THOMAS NELSON
Since 1798